THE CROSSINGS TREASURY OF

Angel Stories

Contemporary Stories of Angelic Encounters

Robert Strand

E**ergreen** PRESS

Published by Crossings Book Club in association with Evergreen Press, Mobile, Alabama.

ISBN 978-1-61664-343-0

Printed in the United States of America

This book is dedicated

to all the wonderful people

who have so willingly shared

their angel stories in the hope

that they will bless and encourage others!

Thanks for your help.

Table of Contents

Section 4 Travel Mercies – Highway to Heaven

Section 5 Blessings and Encouragement – A Wing and a Prayer

Section 6 Missionaries – Angel at My Side

Section 7 Healing and Salvation – Angels to the Rescue

Introduction

There is a great desire today to know more about the spiritual world. In this unseen realm, which is such an integral part of God's universe, we are aware of powerful, exciting, and wonderful forces at work behind the scenes of our reality. People continue to be fascinated with angels, and the hunger for their stories may never be satisfied.

Angels are beings who apparently move faster than the speed of light and can intervene in human affairs both large and small. These affairs may encompass nations or be as small as the concerns of a little child. Most importantly, angels are involved in carrying out the will of their Master—God.

We have been discovering many unique ways in which these wonderful beings perform their ministry. They can stand guard, protect us, convey messages to us, help us, offer comfort when we need it, and engage in cosmic, spiritual battles which we are not even aware are taking place.

Many people unfortunately have been exposed to a lot of misinformation about angels. Too much of this has come from poor resources. There's a lot of angel lore, ancient stories, myths and of course, experiences from people who claim to have had such encounters. Everything you have heard or are reading about angels and their ministry must be measured against the standard of truth—God's Word.

The greatest and most authentic source of angel stories is still the Bible, which contains many incidents dealing with the ministry of angels. The Bible refers to angels as "ministering spirits" (Hebrews 1:14) whom God sends as His messengers to assist people He loves. In fact, if you were to take your Bible concordance and count the mention of angels, you'll see there are approximately 300 of them! It's a huge subject demanding more detailed study.

The biblical accounts of angels in the Book of Acts alone cover ministry from the ascension of Jesus when two angels told the disciples, "this same Jesus" would return once again as He has gone away (Acts 1:11). An angel delivered apostles who had been arrested and placed in prison (Acts 5:19). An angel gave direction to Philip the evangelist as to where he should go (Acts 8:26). Another angel told Cornelius to send for Peter; in fact, he even gave him the address of where he was to go (Acts 10:1-6). When Peter had been imprisoned, an angel set him free, to the surprise of the church which had been praying for his deliverance (Acts 12:1-10). When King Herod failed to give glory to God, an angel brought judgment against him (Acts 12:20-23). These incidents are just a small sampling.

Angelic appearances are usually sudden and without any corroborating witnesses in the vicinity. But the fact that something unusual has happened gives credence to the belief that some kind of angelic ministry has occurred.

The stories that follow are about people, just like you and me, who have had an angelic encounter. The best way to enjoy an angel story is to take it at face value and believe that the source has shared it in all honesty.

An angel story can be enjoyed by all ages. We will explore many aspects of angelic visitors. We'll look at some of the mystery, purpose, and actions of angels as they interact with our fellow human beings! Enjoy! Be thrilled! Be encouraged! And share these with someone who needs encouragement.

—*Robert Strand, Springfield, Missouri, 2010*

PROVISION

Special Delivery Angels

All at once an angel touched him and said,
"Get up and eat" (1 Kings 19:4b-5).

CHAPTER 1

THE HELMET MAKER

While the world was mourning the loss of Princess Diana, one family had its own tragedy. On that August evening, wife and mother Carrie was on her way to visit her parents when an unexpected accident occurred. Shortly after dark, as she carried her nine-month-old son, Stephen Wayne, down a sloping sidewalk, Carrie tripped over the dog and fell on the concrete.

Stephen Wayne was seriously injured in this fall and had a fractured skull. The next few days were filled with tests and waiting for the swelling to subside. Lots of family members and friends were supporting little Stephen with prayers and concern.

On Sunday morning, the doctors concluded that emergency surgery might be needed to find out why the baby's blood count was so low. Blood was being lost somewhere, and he also had bleeding on the brain. Everyone in this family's circle of friends was alerted to pray. The tests came back with a count high enough that surgery was not needed yet.

After several months, the skull fracture was separating instead of closing, and so the decision was made to send little

Stephen Wayne to Cardinal Glennon Children's Medical Center in St. Louis where he had brain surgery. Following this surgery, it was necessary for this little guy to wear a protective helmet for several months to protect his head while healing was taking place.

His parents discovered that these helmets were very expensive, and they had no funds to pay for it. They were directed to make an appointment with a gentleman whose office was in the basement of the medical center. They took Stephen there to have his head measured so the helmet could be custom made. When they returned later to pick up the helmet, the wife asked how much they were to pay for it. They had expected the amount to be several hundred dollars, and they worried how they could possibly cover the cost. To their great surprise the helmet maker said the bill was thirteen dollars—exactly the amount of cash in the wife's purse. What a miracle!

Sometime later when they returned to the hospital to have the stitches removed from the little boy's head, they decided to take a special thank-you note to the helmet maker. They rode the same elevator to the basement and discovered nothing was there—no office, no prosthetic maker! They took the elevator back up and asked the receptionist at the desk if the office of the prosthetic company had moved. She looked at the family in surprise and declared she knew nothing about an office in the basement. She stated that as long as she had been working in the hospital, nothing like that had ever been in the basement. But the family had been there twice—once for the fitting and one time to pick up the helmet.

The only logical conclusion this family reached was that it had been an angel on a very special assignment for them.

By the way, little Stephan Wayne made a complete recovery with no ill effects. He is a very bright teenager today and doing just great!

He will command his angels concerning you, and they will lift you up in their hands, so that you will not strike your foot against a stone (Matthew 4:6).

FOOD FOR THOUGHT: How do you explain such a story? The people are a reliable source with witnesses, so they can't be discredited. The only explanation that seems logical is that it was another angelic intervention in the normal course of human events. But this only works if you have faith. You can pick apart any event, but the truth still remains and demands an answer. Faith makes it make sense.

CHAPTER 2

A CHOCOLATE CAKE TOO

*T*imes were really tough for the pastor of a small church in Knob Noster, Missouri. Because the economy was depressed, the church suffered a significant loss of income. Unemployment was everywhere. In the midst of such a downturn, the pastor tried valiantly to believe that God was their source and would provide for his family. The cupboards in the parsonage were bare, the car had no gas, and no jobs were available.

The pastor walked into his kitchen and casually asked his wife what she was writing as she stared thoughtfully at the empty shelves. Her answer really annoyed him rather than inspired him. She said, "I'm making a shopping list of the things I will buy when the Lord sends the money."

With more than a hint of sarcasm, the young pastor said, "Well as long as you're making a list, put me down for chocolate cake!" Her long slim fingers gripped the pencil stub and jotted down, "chocolate cake." However, after looking at the entry, she crossed it out, thinking it a bit selfish and impractical.

Later that day a car whipped up the drive of the parsonage. When the pastor answered the door, one of the ladies from their church stood holding a large sack of groceries in each arm. "Here," she said, "take these and come back. There's more, and I'm in a hurry because I'm late for work."

Speechless, he hurried to the kitchen and set the sacks of food beside his wife's list. Two more large sacks were waiting for him at the front door. She said, "I can't talk right now, but God told me to share."

Later after her shift at work had ended, she stopped back by the parsonage. Both the giver and recipients recognized they had been participants in a miracle. The pastor's wife wiped away tears as her tale unfolded. She had carefully marked off each item from her "faith" list as she removed the items from the grocery sacks. Every item was there, including the chocolate cake!

The donor then related how she had been told by a voice exactly what to load into the sacks from her own pantry shelves. While she was packing the specified groceries, the chocolate cake mix had toppled down and hit her on the head two times. She placed it back on the shelf each time, and when it hit her on the head the third time, she thought, *Well, Lord, if they want chocolate cake that much, I'll just give it to them with the frosting too!*

With hearts overflowing in gratefulness and full stomachs all around, this little ministry family went to bed that night with a better realization of just how much their heavenly Father loved and cared about them.

And my God will meet all your needs according to his glorious riches in Christ Jesus (Philippians 4:19).

FOOD FOR THOUGHT: It seems as though preachers too need a real life lesson in the goodness and graciousness of God. We are so human, so filled with worry, when all the time we have a heavenly Father who is so concerned about each of us that He numbers the hairs on each of our heads. Hang in there and don't give up. Divine help may be on the way no matter how tough the times are.

CHAPTER 3

THE MONEY ANGEL

*T*his story begins in the early 1970s, in Rockford, Illinois, as Pastor Don Lyons led his church to purchase some farmland on which to build a new church building and a Christian radio station. First, they built a small house, which was to be used for the radio station if they could manage to get it launched. Pastor Lyons knew they needed to find a special person to manage this startup ministry. As the pastor prayed about it, in his mind, he could see a name spelled out: "Tietsort." *A most unusual name,* he thought. Shaking his head, he quickly dismissed it from his mind.

Some time later, at a special pastor's meeting for all the churches in Rockford, Pastor Lyons was greeting some of the guests when a young man walked up. The pastor couldn't believe his eyes when he saw the man's name tag, which read: RON TIETSORT. Pastor Lyons soon discovered that Ron had a radio/television background before he became a pastor in Sioux City, Iowa. Pastor Lyons immediately told the man his story and offered Ron the job of station manager so they could finally get the proposed station on the air. The Tietsort family soon moved to Rockford.

Ron's wife, Millie, became the bookkeeper, receptionist, and occasional programmer. Then in the winter of 1975, reality had to be faced. Despite all their efforts and a growing listener base, the radio station was in deep financial trouble. In order to catch up on their bills and keep it going, the station immediately needed a little more than $3,000, although it might as well have been three million! (Remember at that time a dollar was worth much more than today, and $3,000 seemed like a fortune to them.)

By then they had exhausted all possible avenues for fresh revenue. Millie sat looking out the window at the softly falling snow—a beautiful, refreshing sight. She prayed, "Lord, we really thought You wanted the station to succeed. Did we misread You? Please tell us what to do now."

The front door swung open and a middle-aged man walked in, carrying a sealed envelope. Millie was startled at the sudden intrusion since she had heard no car drive up nor footsteps on the porch. *Perhaps,* she thought, *the snow had muffled the sounds.*

The man said quickly, "Give this to Ron. Use it for the station."

Before Millie could offer him a receipt for tax purposes, he turned and quickly left. Gone! It seemed so strange that the man never engaged in any further conversation with her.

Millie hurried to Ron's office and excitedly plopped the bulging envelope in front of him. With a quizzical look on his face, Ron slit the envelope, opened it, and gasped. "Millie, look!" The envelope was stuffed with money. They quickly began counting it and found the envelope contained $3,250!

Ron leaped from his chair, raced to the front of the house, and flung open the door to call the man back so he could thank him or at least meet him. But there was no car in sight, no tire tracks in the driveway—none coming from the road and none going back out! Then Ron looked down the front walkway and saw there were also no footprints! He looked at the fresh snow on the unshoveled front porch, and it was completely smooth. No impressions to be seen anywhere on the fresh white carpet of clean snow!

Well, what about today? Yes, Station WQFL and its companion station of WGLS are still operating!

And Ron and Millie never saw the stranger again, but how well they remember him.

H.C. Moolenburgh wrote, "The farther we go along the path of God, the more angels we shall encounter."

And my God will meet all your needs according to his glorious riches in Christ Jesus (Philippians 4:19).

FOOD FOR THOUGHT: If you are a Bible student, you no doubt have discovered impressive evidence of what angels did throughout the biblical accounts. But you may be thinking, *What evidence is there today that angels are still doing such things?* The place to start is with the character of God who has His reasons for creating angels (as well as you and me), and they all come from who He is!

CHAPTER 4

AN ANGELIC HOUSEKEEPER

Gladys Triplett scarcely had enough strength to answer the doorbell that morning in 1941 in Newberg, Oregon. Not fully recovered from the birth of their eighth child, she had spent a sleepless night and although it was only about 10:30 a.m., she was already exhausted. She felt too weak to tackle the mountain of dirty dishes, the unmade beds, and the huge pile of laundry. Rev. Triplett, her husband, was absent, being the speaker for a special meeting in another city. To Gladys, it all seemed too much to handle.

When the plainly dressed woman at the door used the word "prayer," Gladys, in her fatigue, thought she had come to receive prayer. Instead the visitor reassured her, "No, no, I did not come for prayer. The Father has sent me to minister to you, dear child, because of your distress and great need. You called with all your heart, and you asked in faith."

Then, lifting Gladys in her arms the stranger laid her on the couch and said, "Your heavenly Father heard your prayer. Sleep now, my child, for He cares for you."

When Gladys awoke refreshed three hours later, she

11

stared in amazement at the change in her house. All the children's belongings had been picked up and the floors were cleaned. Her baby, three months old, had been bathed and was asleep.

The dining room table, extended to its full length, was spread with the best tablecloth and set with her finest table service. She was especially surprised to see it was set for thirteen people. The stranger explained, "Oh, you will be having guests soon."

Even more astounding was the appearance of the kitchen. The heaps of dirty dishes were gone; there was a freshly baked cake, a large bowl of salad, as well as other prepared food on the counter. Later, the family learned that even the cooking utensils had been washed.

Most surprising of all was what had happened to the laundry. The basket of baby clothes, a full hamper of family laundry, and all the bedding had been washed, dried, ironed and put away. The guest was just folding up the ironing board.

How could all this be accomplished? The washing machine could not possibly have put out that many loads in three hours. Furthermore, Gladys didn't own a dryer, and it was raining outside; but nevertheless, the clothes were dried.

Gladys knew that three basketfuls of ironing usually took her almost two days to complete, yet the visitor had done it, along with everything else, all in one morning. Later, Gladys discovered that every bed had been changed and made, and each child's clothing had been folded and put in the proper drawer.

When the children came home from school, they noticed something unusual about their visitor. Puzzled, some of the younger ones whispered, "Who is she, Mama? She looks kind of different."

Gladys explained, "This is a wonderful friend God sent to help me today."

Gladys suddenly realized that her fatigue was gone, her body completely healed, and she felt stronger than she had in years! She attempted to learn more about this friendly helper who would simply say, "Just say I am a friend or child of God who came because of your prayer."

Shortly after the kids arrived home, Rev. Triplett unexpectedly returned. The meetings had been interrupted because of a death at the host church. With him were five others: the pastor, his wife, and another couple and their daughter. When they sat down to eat dinner, there were exactly thirteen people were at the table! The meal was the most delicious any of them could remember.

After the mysterious visitor had met Rev. Triplett and just before the family sat down at the table, she quietly slipped out the door.

Who was she? No human being could have done so much in so little time, have known where to put each child's clothing, or been aware of the exact number of people that would be present for dinner. The family questioned many people, neighbors, friends, and even the police. No one could offer a clue as to her identity!

"I have had enough, Lord," he said. "Take my life; I am no better than my ancestors." Then he lay down under the tree and fell asleep. All at once an angel touched him and said, 'Get up and eat'" (I Kings 19:4b-5).

FOOD FOR THOUGHT: Imagine…an angel doing housework! But, then again, why not? We usually think of them as being warriors and involved in huge projects. Why not be involved in the mundane, even in housework? It's a refreshing, perhaps new concept of angels at work among us.

CHAPTER 5

MODERN MANNA

*N*ewlyweds John and Bonnie Eller had been serving at their first pastorate for only six weeks. At this moment they were facing a difficult financial situation. Their small church in northeast Arkansas was not able to support a full-time pastor. John had looked for employment at every business in the small town of 1,700 people but had not been offered a job.

That evening Bonnie had served the last of their food supply—pancakes made with water and sweetened with their last teaspoon of sugar. "This is all we have, John," said Bonnie. "But don't worry, God called us here, and He won't let us down."

However, the young husband was understandably worried. He had never faced a situation like this before. When he went to bed, he tossed and turned for several hours. Finally, he arose, went to the living room, and turned on the light. Then he did something he would not normally recommend. Sitting on their threadbare couch, he held his Bible in his hands and let it fall open where it would. Instantly his eyes fell on a verse that stated, "It is God who arms me with strength and makes my way perfect" (2 Samuel 22:33). That settled the matter for the young pastor. He returned to bed and almost immediately fell asleep.

The next morning, about six o'clock, there was a loud knock at the side door of the humble little parsonage. Hurriedly putting on his bathrobe, John opened the door.

Standing at the doorstep was a very elderly man holding two large grocery sacks in his arms. He was wearing a faded red flannel shirt and bib overalls. Thin, stooped and unshaven, he was carrying a walking cane in the crook of his arm.

"Here, preacher," he said in a hoarse and trembling voice, "you may need these."

Reaching out with both arms, John hugged the two heavy sacks together and carried them toward the little mohair chair in the living room. Placing them there, he turned around to thank his benefactor, but he was gone!

Excited, the pastor ran outside and looked up and down the street. The man was nowhere in sight! John ran around the house and over to the church next door, but there was no trace of the man who had been there moments before.

Returning to the house, John found Bonnie smiling with big tears rolling down her cheeks. She had gone into the living room to examine the contents of the sacks. To her amazement, she found everything they normally would buy: two large cans of pineapple juice, sugar, flour, canned vegetables, meat, and even their favorite brand of coffee!

"See," Bonnie exclaimed, "I told you God would take care of us. He even knows what brands we like."

After breakfast John went through the town's tiny business district, describing the man who had brought the groceries and asking if anyone knew him. Everyone answered in the negative; no such man had ever been seen in their community.

During the remainder of their time as pastors in that little town, the Ellers often inquired about the man who had brought help to them in their time of need. They never saw nor heard of him again.

Since then, the Ellers have never found themselves in such dire circumstances, but they have remained confident that the Lord who helped them that time would always supply their needs.

I was young and now I am old, yet I have never seen the righteous forsaken or their children begging bread (Psalm 37:25).

FOOD FOR THOUGHT: What an exciting example of God's love, care, and provision for His own! Never too soon, never too late…but timed to the tick of a clock and the beat of a heart, God's provision will be there!

CHAPTER 6

CHICKEN ON THE DOORKNOB

The following story happened to Leon Miles and his wife when they were rookie pastors in their first church whose people had all kinds of needs.

We discovered just how needy the church was when we were handed our first weekly paycheck—it was made out to us in the princely sum of $3.85. We were struck with the question of how we would be able to eat and support our little family.

Discouraged as we were and yet optimistic as beginners are about the future, we thanked the Lord for the $3.85. But we also began praying with a bit of desperation about our future and the basics of life. We decided it would be nice if we could at least eat. However, we began to believe and pray on the promises of Proverbs 3:5-6 and the promise of Matthew 6:33.

God began to prove Himself the very next day, which was a Monday. A person dropped by at 6:00 a.m. with cereal and milk for the family. At noon, meat arrived in the form of steaks to go along with the vegetables that had earlier that morning been dropped by our humble upstairs apartment.

On the following Saturday, a weekly occurrence began that lasted until the day we moved. When the doorbell rang, I shouted down the stairway, "Come on in." No response. So down the steps I went to check it out, but there was no one around. So I retraced my steps up the stairs. When I got back up to our floor in the four-unit apartment building, I saw the best fryer chicken one could buy in our town hanging on the doorknob.

For the next five years, the doorbell would ring some time every Saturday, and when we went to answer, no one would be there. It happened every single Saturday, always at different times, but without fail. It happened when we had guests or when we had none, or when we were in special meetings or just had regular Sunday services. When it rained or when it snowed or when it was nice, regular as clockwork there would be a bag hanging on the doorknob with meat inside. But we never caught a glimpse of who brought it.

Inside the bag, always wrapped in butcher paper, would be a ham, steaks, roasts, chickens, fish, etc. It was always something meeting the needs of our growing family plus any guests we were going to have that week. Who could be the angel delivering this beautiful package and how could he or she disappear so quickly?

Time passed and finally it was our last Saturday at this parish. The doorbell rang. I assumed it was the mysterious visitor, so I ran down the steps to get to the front door as quickly as possible. I caught sight of a taxi cab, with no passengers, pulling away from the curb.

We looked at the last package to discover it had come from the town's best meat market and had been sent "special delivery" by taxi. We then assumed that all the meats had come from this source. We inquired at the market, only to be told they knew nothing about the mysterious happenings. To this day we have no clue as to whom God used to provide the meats. All we know is that He did, and we were sustained. We had been fed for five years, and we never went hungry!

All at once an angel touched him and said, "Get up and eat." He looked around, and there by his head was a cake of bread baked over hot coals, and a jar of water. He ate and drank and then lay down again. The angel of the Lord came back a second time and touched him and said, "Get up and eat, for the journey is too much for you." So he got up and ate and drank. Strengthened by that food, he traveled forty days and forty nights... (1 Kings 19:5-8).

FOOD FOR THOUGHT: In a desert scene we see Elijah, and we're all surprised at what he finds—a fire of hot coals, a pan of bread baking over it with a toasty, brown crust, and the delicious aroma to tell him it's ready to eat! Besides that, there was a pottery jar of cool, clear water with beads of moisture running down the outside. Amazing! Where did angels learn how to bake bread? Or that humans need cool water to drink? Or that humans need sleep and rest?

CHAPTER 7

THE SKINNY LITTLE ANGEL

A number of years ago I was a speaker at a morning prayer group, which meets in a town near Springfield, Illinois. Before I spoke, a neighboring pastor shared with us about his recent trip to Mexico.

Along with several others, the pastor had gone to Mexico on a preaching mission. While they were returning, their van developed mechanical problems. After jacking up the van, the pastor crawled underneath to check out the problem. Suddenly the jack collapsed, and he felt the crushing weight of the van on his chest! His companions quickly grabbed the bumper to attempt to lift the van, but they were unable to budge it.

He cried out, "Jesus! Jesus!" with what little remaining breath he had. Within seconds a youthful looking man came running toward them. He was quite thin, skinny even, and small in stature. He was smiling as he approached them. When he reached the van, he grabbed the bumper and lifted the van by himself! It was as though the van was a feather in his hands.

As he was freed of the weight of the van, the pastor felt his chest expand and the crushed, broken ribs immediately mend! He crawled out from under the van in his own strength.

The visitor then lowered the van, waved to them and ran back in the same direction from which he had come and simply disappeared on the horizon as they watched. No one knew who the mysterious visitor was or where he had come from!

Then King Nebuchadnezzar leaped to his feet in amazement and asked his advisors, "Weren't there three men that we tied up and threw into the fire?" They replied, "Certainly, O king." He said, "Look! I see four men walking around in the fire, unbound and unharmed, and the fourth looks like a son of the gods" (Daniel 3:24-25).

FOOD FOR THOUGHT: A traditional song contains this line: "All night, all day, angels watching over me, my Lord." Yes, and I believe this is more than a song—it's a biblical truth that is comforting to all who might be in distress, in need, or in danger!

CHAPTER 8

THE ANGEL PROMISED

*S*amuel Doctorian is an Armenian, born in Beirut. He became a Christian in Jerusalem as a teenager. He's a fascinating man who has traveled the Middle East sharing his story of conversion in places such as Lebanon, Israel, Egypt, Jordan, Syria, Greece, and Cyprus. The following is his exciting story:

One night after a meeting, I was sitting with James Osmand and his wife, Liberty, at their kitchen table. They were sharing with me their sorrow about having lost three children. And the saddest part, Liberty shared with tears, was that doctors now had said that having another child was not possible.

She said, "I'm so sorry I've lost three, but the worst is I will not have any more children. I'd love to have another child."

Of course I felt sorry for them and prayed with them. Then about eleven o'clock, I retired for the night. I prepared for bed and fell on my knees to pray. As I was praying, suddenly an angel of the Lord came and stood right in front of me in the bedroom! I saw him in full bright light. He had a glorious face and a wonderful smile. He came with a scroll in his hand and did not speak. He opened the scroll, and I read the words from the Lord. It was a clear message: "Go and tell my daughter, I shall give her a son next year."

You can imagine my joy and excitement. I quickly put on my robe and ran downstairs. They were still in the kitchen talking together and weeping. Jim was trying to comfort his wife.

I came in with great excitement and said, "Liberty, I have a message for you. The Lord just now sent an angel to my room."

She shouted: "What! An angel? Right here?"

I said, "Yes. He just came in my room while I was praying. And this is the message, Liberty. 'Next year at this time you shall have a son.'"

Can you imagine the tremendous joy of that night? I don't remember what time we went to bed, but we all rejoiced and praised the Lord for this glorious message that the angel had brought.

Oh, yes, you must also know this: exactly one year later—to the day—a son was born to James and Liberty Osmand!

Awesome! The story didn't end there. Eighteen years later I was in England attending a "League of Prayer" convention with Jim Osmand, who was one of the special speakers. Liberty and Jim were happy to see me, but their greatest joy was for me to meet their son, the promised one. He was eighteen years old and a very dedicated Christian. How thrilling it was to see him, hug him, and praise God for the glorious and wonderful fulfillment of the message that the angel brought to me in the upstairs bedroom, eighteen years before! Hallelujah!

In the sixth month, God sent the angel Gabriel to Nazareth, a town in Galilee, to a virgin pledged to be married to a man named Joseph, a descendant of David. The virgin's name was Mary. The angel went to her and said, "Greetings, you who are highly favored! The Lord is with you." Mary was greatly troubled at his words and wondered what kind of greeting this might be. But the angel said to her, "Do not be afraid, Mary, you have found favor with God. You will be with child and give birth to a son, and you are to give him the name Jesus" (Luke 1:26-31).

FOOD FOR THOUGHT: Why not another announcement of a pending birth by an angel? Think of some of these same kinds of announcements in the Bible—an angel announced the births of Isaac, Samson, Samuel, John the Baptist, and of course Jesus Christ, as well as others. Can you imagine the excitement in the hearts of the parents who received such news? What a blessing!

CHAPTER 9

AN ANGEL FOR AN ANGELL

"Hi, my name is Angell, Judith Angell," she said as she introduced herself to me. We had stopped at a craft and gift shop in one of Missouri's top tourist spots. I couldn't believe my ears.

"Would you be so kind as to repeat that?" I asked.

"Sure," she said, with a smile this time, "my name is Judith Angell."

I was intrigued because I'm always on the lookout for another angel story worth sharing with my readers. And it's amazing where these stories have come from and how they have been shared and eventually end up in print.

So I pressed on, "Surely there's some kind of an angel story connected with your having a name like that."

She smiled some more and replied, "Yes, I get asked something like that all the time. Why did you ask?"

"I'm a writer and I'm always on the alert for another story for the next book I have been commissioned to write about angel encounters," was my answer.

"Well, what kind of a book are you writing?"

"This is the third in the series of stories. In fact, I've just done a book signing in the area and happen to have a sample. If you'll wait, I'll run out to the car and show you the format and leave a copy with you." I brought back the book *Angel at My Door* and discussed what I need in an angel story.

She replied, "Okay, I'll share it." And she proceeded to tell me the following story.

This story happened just a few short days ago. I have worked all over the world with a major investment company and took an early retirement. I'm single so I can live almost any place in the world, but I chose this area and bought myself a working horse ranch. I raise registered horses and train them. It's something I've always wanted to do, and I found the exact ranch I desired.

One day, as I looked over my yearling herd, I couldn't find a particular stallion. He was missing, and I immediately became alarmed. So I set out on foot looking for him in the pasture where he was supposed to be. Now my ranch covers more than one thousand acres, so this could be a long search. I made my way to the very back of the ranch and found him tangled up in the fence! When he saw me, he whinnied and looked at me with fear in his eyes. Somehow he had managed to get both front feet tangled up in the barbed wire fence.

By this time I was a long way from my barns, house and help. It would take me more than an hour to go for help and return. Fortunately, he was standing quietly, not moving, but you could see where the barbs had ripped into his legs, and the blood was dripping. I just sat down in frustration and began to cry. *What could I do? Who would help? If I left him, would he injure himself more? Would he panic if I left?*

27

All of a sudden I heard a voice, "Judith, get up!" I looked around, but nobody could be seen. Was I hearing things? Then again I heard, "Judith, get up!" louder this time. I was really thinking that I might be losing it, so I still sat there. Once more, "JUDITH, GET UP!" This time I obeyed, but I wasn't sure what to do.

Then came further instructions: "Get under the horse and lift up his front legs, and you will get him out of the fence." So I scrambled under him, placed my head between his two front legs and began to lift up against his chest. Now when you think about this, it's ridiculous. There I was, a woman in my early sixties, not weighing more than 110 pounds, attempting to lift a nearly full-grown horse! But as I straightened my back and lifted upwards holding his two legs with my hands, he came loose and was suddenly freed! I dropped to my hands and knees while he stood still and crawled out from under him.

Where had the voice and the instructions come from? The only conclusion I have is that an angel came to my rescue! The little stallion? He quickly recovered with no scars or lasting injuries.

The angel of the Lord asked him, "Why have you beaten your donkey these three times. . . . The donkey saw me and turned away from me these three times" (Numbers 22:32-33).

FOOD FOR THOUGHT: Do you think the Lord is interested enough in an animal to send an angel to help with the rescue? Why not? An angel was totally involved with the prophet Balaam and his donkey in the above scripture. Why not read the entire incident found in Numbers 22:21-44?

CHAPTER 10

THE DELIVERY ANGEL

As I look back, I realize that my growing up years were wonderful and idyllic, and I had a really happy childhood. It never dawned on me that life was really tough at times because we were so poor. At this time, my parents were struggling to establish a mission church in west central Minnesota in the town of Evansville, which had a population of about 750 people, not counting dogs and cats. It was not easy to make a living in those days. In addition to being a pioneering pastor, Dad had to work where he could find a job to support the family. Our family consisted of Dad, Mom, my younger brother Gene, who was a year and half my junior, and myself. We had a little garden and ate well when some of the church farm families brought some of their produce to the parsonage. I thought everybody had to live like that, but the memories of those years are good. It's amazing what time can do to memory.

However, one particular night is still a vivid memory. Mom was setting the table for herself and us two boys when Gene asked, "What are we going to eat tonight?" We had al-

29

ready checked and knew that nothing was on the stove or in the refrigerator and cupboards, and nothing was on the table except water in the glasses. We didn't even have one potato to make watery soup or any flour with which to make biscuits. There were no noodles for a hot dish of any kind. The house was bare, and two boys were famished!

Mother said, "Let's sit down and ask the Lord to bless our meal." We dutifully bowed our heads and listened to her prayer: "Dear Lord, we thank you because You are so good to us. Bless Dad tonight as he's away working. And, Lord, thank You for the food we are about to partake of, in Jesus' name I pray…" Before she said the final "Amen," all three of us heard a noise on the back porch. Being boys, we shoved our chairs back and in a single motion ran for the back door, which was about six steps from the kitchen table, and flung it open. There, sitting on the porch, were boxes of groceries! We ran out onto the porch and down the three steps, looking in every direction up and down our little dirt street. We saw nobody, no car driving away, nothing! Now this is a little country village where everybody knew everybody and everybody knew everybody else's business. We could see quite a distance in all directions, and we could see no one.

You can imagine the great excitement as we hauled the groceries inside, helping Mom put them away until they overflowed the cupboards and the refrigerator! Then we sat down to a glorious feast! We asked, "Mom, who do you think brought the groceries?"

She looked back with a smile and simply said, "Let's just thank the Lord for providing!"

We experienced other instances of miraculous provision during those same years. Many times some anonymous giver would drop a plain envelope into our mailbox with fifty dollars in it along with a note that simply said: "Let not your right hand know what your left hand is doing." These envelopes always arrived when we were in the middle of a financial crisis. It was an ongoing event that happened many times during those years, and they were always delivered on the very day we needed them. Eventually my brother and I set up a watch over our mailbox to catch the person or persons who did it, but we never saw anyone put the envelopes in that box.

Rabbah, an ancient Jewish scholar wrote: "Although the span from earth to heaven is a journey of five hundred years, when one whispers a prayer, or even silently meditates, God is nearby and hears."

I was young and now I am old, yet I have never seen the righteous forsaken or their children begging bread (Psalm 37:25).

FOOD FOR THOUGHT: Angels exist for a reason—they are servants of God. They have work to do and apparently always will. Angels exist in numbers so huge they cannot be counted and will be there throughout eternity. Does this give us a hint that heaven will be a busy place with lots of action because God Himself will be setting the pace?

PROTECTION

Guardians From on High

For it is written: "He will command his angels concerning you to guard you carefully" (Luke 4:10).

CHAPTER 11

THE HELP-ME-UP ANGELS

*B*etty returned home following a visit to her sister at about 5:45 pm on New Year's Day. Here's her story:

Because of a previous mugging experience, I have made it a habit not to get out of my car if men are walking in the street or if only one car is riding through our cul-de-sac. I have to see either two or more cars or none at all before I will get out of the car.

Well, two cars were coming around our circle, so I climbed out of my car. The first car stopped next to my car, and the driver asked for directions, which was not unusual. There wasn't room for the second car to pass because a third car was parked on the other side of the narrow street. (Thank you, God!) The man who asked for directions left, and I walked up to my house. My door has two locks, and before I put the key into the first lock, the driver who had asked directions completed the circle again and pulled into the driveway behind my car. My first thought was that the car had come for the lady who lives upstairs. Then I heard him yell out the street name he had asked me about earlier.

I knew better than to go back down the stairs to the waiting car, but something kept telling me to do it anyway, so I finally did. I stood at the passenger side and looked into the window. The man asked additional questions politely and even thanked me. Then he pulled a gun and stuck it in my face, telling me to put my purse on the seat. I told him I only had five dollars, and I'd give it to him but not my purse since there wasn't anything else in it that he could use. I wasn't going to go to the expense of buying a new purse and obtaining a replacement driver's license. He yelled at me to put my purse in the car or he would shoot me. I got so mad I said, "That's it!" I turned and walked away.

Our driveway is steep, like a ramp, and when I started to walk up it, I tripped and fell. I didn't have my cane with me, and I knew I couldn't get up. The driver obviously didn't care that I might be hurt and need help. I felt like he was going to shoot me in the back, but I was so mad I didn't care. It seemed like he was there forever with the gun trained on my back, but again I was so mad I didn't care. "Go ahead and shoot me!" I screamed and kept yelling until he took off. I continued shouting for help because I couldn't get up. I was so upset I thought I'd have a heart attack from the anger.

Nobody heard my screams so no one came to help me. Then suddenly I was standing up tall and straight on both feet. I had come up like a feather. One moment I was lying on the ground in some pain and crying out for help, and the next, I was on my feet, experiencing no more pain, and a peace and calmness came over my spirit.

My conclusion is that only angels could have helped me. In front of my house is a street light that was installed after I had been mugged previously, but my porch is very dark. If I had been accosted on the porch, no one would have seen him, and it would have been possible for him to enter my house. I believe it was an angel who urged me to walk back down the drive into the light, preventing the man from coming after me because he knew his actions could have been easily seen.

My sister doesn't believe the story about the angels, but I know better.

I tell you, there is rejoicing in the presence of the angels of God over one sinner who repents (Luke 15:10).

FOOD FOR THOUGHT: Many of these angel stories are about angels helping people in seemingly impossible situations. I'm always amazed at the variety of stories shared with me. Some of them make believers out of others. Our relationship to God is based on faith, so the choice is simply to believe or not. There are no in between shades.

CHAPTER 12

SHE'S CHOKING!

*R*ene is our storyteller in this chapter. She tells about an angelic encounter her mother had that saved her life.

My mother met my father when she was fifteen and he was nineteen. They dated for three years and married when she was eighteen. Mom became pregnant a month later and gave birth to my sister, June. This happened during the Great Depression. A few years later, they had a baby boy who was named after my father, Ernie. The baby contracted an infection and died when he was only three months old.

About four years later, they had another baby boy and again named him after my father. Something was wrong with him because he cried most of the time even though the doctors couldn't find the cause. My mother would walk the floor with him every night. She needed to keep him as quiet as possible so my father could get some sleep since he had to get up very early for work.

One morning when he was almost a year old, my mother woke with a start and realized the baby had not awakened her with his crying during the night. She rushed to his room and found him dead in his crib. The doctor said he had died of internal convulsions. This time my parents were inconsolable with grief. They were so poor they had to bury my brother in an orange crate. They were so devastated by this second death that all they could do was cling together and try to carry on for my sister's sake. My mother would walk to the store, and if she saw any of the ladies that had been in the hospital maternity ward with her, she would cross the street so she would not have to look at their babies.

By the time my sister became a teenager, my mother couldn't stop wanting another baby. My father did not think it was a good idea, but she persisted and became pregnant with me. When I was born, she was extremely overprotective with me to the point that she wouldn't allow anyone else in the kitchen when she sterilized my formula.

By this time we had moved into a nice older house with a large front covered porch the length of the house. One day when I was nine months old, my mother sat me in my high chair on the porch to have lunch. She had cut some roast beef finely and ground it with a spoon into tiny pieces that I could eat. All at once I started to choke on the beef, which had become clogged in my throat, shutting off my airway. My mother picked me up and frantically began to pray, "Lord, not again! Lord help me quickly; help me now!"

I was the precious answer to her prayers, and she could not bear the thought of anything bad happening to me. I was starting to show signs of serious oxygen deprivation and stiffened in her arms. She became even more frantic! Suddenly a very bright ray of light shown down through the roof of the porch. She said, "It was brighter than any sunlight I have ever seen." Then a voice came from the light and instructed her to hit me on the back as hard as she could. She obeyed and the meat that had been stuck in my throat popped out. I could breathe again! She later recounted this story to me when I was old enough to understand it. She said she believed that Jesus or an angel had come to save my life.

The Spirit sent him out into the desert, and he was in the desert forty days...and angels attended him (Mark 1:12-13).

FOOD FOR THOUGHT: Here's another situation in which any kind of delay in providing help would have meant certain death to this infant. Is it possible that each of us has at least one guardian angel who is on guard all the time? I am encouraged to know that help can be provided that quickly.

CHAPTER 13

ANGELIC PROTECTION

*B*ecause of the sensitivity of the following story, the names as well as the location have been eliminated.

This particular household had a very abusive husband. The abuse had been verbal but had not yet escalated to the physical level. The woman had become a Christian and began attending a church on a regular basis. The husband became more furious each time she left home and attended a service. She was faithful to attending on Sunday mornings as well as mid-week services. He berated her mercilessly, elevating the derogatory words until finally he forbade her to go to church anymore.

Despite what he had said, she chose to attend church the following Sunday evening. In the middle of the service, her husband drove up to the church with his tires squealing. He marched inside, grabbed his wife by the arm, and escorted her outside. The church overheard him shouting at her that he was going to put an end to her worthless life by shooting her that very night.

The church immediately began to pray for her protection.

While he drove her home, he told her again how he was going to kill her with the gun he had already purchased. He gleefully proclaimed that as soon as they arrived home, the deed would be done.

He pulled into the driveway and rushed into the house to retrieve his gun. The woman's brother was a local county sheriff, and she knew if she could get to a phone, he'd quickly come to her aid. She cautiously made her way into the house to make the call. As she stepped into the hallway, an audible voice said, "Stand still, and I will protect you!"

She stopped in her tracks. As she later said, it was as if a sheet came down around her and completely covered her. She heard her husband load the gun and come searching for her. He walked right past his wife, not seeing her, and searched for her in the car and around the outside of the house. When he came back inside, he walked right past her again. Finally, he gave up trying to find her. She heard him unload his gun, drop his shoes, and lay down on the bed.

The voice spoke again, "Go to bed, and I will protect you." The protective shield/sheet disappeared, and she went to bed. She later described her evening, "What a peaceful night of rest I had." She woke once in the night, and the voice repeated, "I will protect you."

The next morning her husband angrily said, "Where did you go last night to hide? I couldn't find you. Then this morning I got up to try to shoot you, but a person was protecting you. He told me never ever to harm you again. Who is he? He told me that if I ever harmed you again, he would take care of me. He was real scary."

The following Sunday she told her story to the church and thanked them for their prayers. Her husband never abused her or attempted to kill her again. Eventually he too became a Christian and later told the preacher, "There was a time when I hated my wife and wanted to kill her and you too, but somehow I now love you both."

For it is written: "He will command his angels concerning you to guard you carefully" (Luke 4:10).

FOOD FOR THOUGHT: God is concerned about all our lives, even when domestic violence comes to a home. The Bible promised that God sees the sparrow that falls and numbers the hairs of our head. God is not interested in all our situations. He's a God of the detail; He's a God of compassion; He's a comfort in times of need; He's a friend that is closer than a brother. He has resources to meet every kind of need—even domestic ones.

CHAPTER 14

THE ANGEL IN THE WINDOW

*E*vangelist Frankie Walker related the following story to me while I was doing research on angelic visits:

For a season of time, I was removed from my traveling ministry and taught in a Bible school, did some counseling, and was a dorm mother to some twenty girls.

One evening I had to leave the girls for about an hour and a half to pick up a lady who was traveling from another state to visit our church. The night was extremely dark as I drove out of the parking lot. When I was a short distance away from the dorm, I sensed a strong presence of fear and the thought came, *I cannot leave the girls alone.* I prayed, "Lord, what am I to do? I can't go back; someone has to go to the airport." The Lord impressed me to "charge the angels to guard the dorm." I did this, committing the safety of the girls to the angels.

On arrival back at the dorm, Pastor Eula and I walked into what should have been a sleeping group of young women. Instead we found all of them seated on the floor, singing and worshipping. The girl in charge met me at the top of the stairs. "I know we are supposed to be in bed, but allow me to tell you why we are not. After you left, we were visiting when another student came home from work. She said, 'Why is Sister Walker standing in her window, curtains open, looking out on the parking lot? She never does that; her curtains are always closed at night.' We laughed at her as we explained she must be seeing things because you had gone to the airport."

She paused to catch her breath and then went on: "We continued talking and then the second carload came from work, the same three girls who ride together each day. One of them asked, 'What is Sister Walker doing with her curtains open, watching the parking lot?' At this, the rest of the girls freaked out, some of them frightened to the point of tears."

They then decided to check into my room. They found the lights off and the drapes closed, just as I had left them. Assured that everything was okay, but still shaken, they began to sing and pray together. All of this had been related to me with eyes wide with excitement and some tears.

I told them about my experience on the road as I was leaving the parking lot and the instructions to place angels to guard them in my absence. This was a wonderful opportunity to explain about the supernatural protection of angels and I said, "That angel looked like me and was guarding you while I was absent."

James Russell Lowell once wrote: "An angel stood and met my gaze, through the low doorway of my tent; the tent is struck, the vision stays; I only know she came and went."

So Peter was kept in prison, but the church was earnestly praying to God for him.... "You're out of your mind," they told her. When she kept insisting that it was so, they said, "It must be his angel" (Acts 12:5,15).

FOOD FOR THOUGHT: God is sovereign and does what He wants to do, and He does it the way He wants it done. He may use an angel to perform some service at a moment in time. At another time He may use a word of encouragement through a total stranger, and the next use a Christian friend to do a kind deed. Let's never stop praying for His help in times of need!

CHAPTER 15

THE GIANT ANGEL

*T*his story is from Ralph Nicol, a missionary to Mexico. It happened on a state blacktop road on a dark, foggy night in East Texas.

After a church service on a Wednesday night, a man with whom I had been acquainted for a few years approached me with a problem. He needed help in moving his furniture and belongings from his house in Livingston to another house in Chanal View a few miles away, and he knew I had a truck. We drove over to his house and loaded it up with about three hours of hard, sweaty work. By this time I was more than a bit anxious to get on the road and hoped to be back home before morning.

I was in a real hurry as I drove out of Livingston, driving much too fast for the conditions. It was a foggy night, but we were making pretty good time. All I could see was the white center strip and the line on the side of the road that marked where the shoulder began. Yes, it was foolish. Yes, I was going too fast for the conditions. Yes, I was in too much of a hurry.

Yes, I knew better, but my desire to get home overcame my sense of caution.

Suddenly, standing directly ahead in the middle of the road, looking back at me over his shoulder was a huge man! He had on bright clothing that glowed through the fog. He was huge and towered over the hood of my truck. I would estimate that he must have been about nine or ten feet tall. He stood still, watching me come up the road. I slammed on the brakes, and the truck burned rubber as it slid to a screeching halt almost on top of him. He smiled at me, and then as we watched, he vanished into thin air, disappearing in an instant! Then it hit both of us—this was an angel on an assignment!

I put the truck in first gear and started down the road, slowly this time, hoping to catch another look at this angel. It was then that we saw a stalled log truck about 100 yards ahead, spread across both sides of the highway. This truck must have pulled out from a side road and stalled, cutting off both lanes of traffic. No flares had yet been put out by the driver because it had just happened. Yes, we were shook up!

I stepped out of the truck and inquired whether the driver needed help, but he was soon able to start the log truck up and pulled it to the side of the road. Curious, I went over and asked him if he had seen this strange man. He had not, but he enjoyed the story as I told it to him.

As my friend and I started up the road again, this time at a much reduced speed, we were talking excitedly about our encounter with a life-saving angel. Soon we were praising God and worshipping the One who cared enough about us, even in the midst of our foolishness, to send protection in a time of dire need. Now don't any of you take this as a license to do something foolish in the belief that God will come to your rescue. I don't know why He spared me and my furniture moving friend, but perhaps God had more for us to do to help His kingdom.

Even though I walk through the valley of the shadow of death, I will fear no evil, for you are with me; your rod and your staff, they comfort me (Psalm 23:4).

FOOD FOR THOUGHT: Angels don't come to judge us. Their mission is to help and protect us. Sometimes we do foolish things and God sends them to rescue us out of our own folly.

CHAPTER 16

ANGEL WARNINGS

*G*enevieve wrote the following letter to me:

I received your book, *In the Company of Angels,* as a Christmas present. And I sure believe in angels. Let me tell you what happened to my sister, Anna.

Anna was sitting in her living room and wanted to get up for a drink of water. All of a sudden, she heard a voice tell her, "Don't go into the bathroom." She looked at her dog, Dagger, and wondered who was talking. So she thought, *I won't go into the bathroom; I'll go into the kitchen and get a drink.*

As she was returning to the living room to sit down, all of a sudden lightning struck in her hall and bathroom. She waited a moment and went to investigate. The electricity didn't work in the bathroom, and the light fixtures showed some damage. She knew immediately that an angel had protected her with his warning. Anna lived in DeSoto, Missouri, where it's really unusual for lightning to strike.

She called her landlord who sent an electrician to repair

the damage. He said, "Anna, where were you when the lightning struck?"

She replied, "Maybe you'll think I'm crazy" and related to him the warning she had received.

He said, "Anna, if you would have been in your bathroom, the lightning would have hit you!"

All she could reply was, "Thank you, Jesus!"

Genevieve went on to relate her own angel story:

Now let me share with you what once happened to me. I had just returned to my apartment from downtown, locked the door behind me, and shut off my radio. (I always leave my radio on when I'm away from home.) After I sat down, I offered thanks to God for another safe shopping trip.

Then a loud rap sounded at my door. My thought was, *I didn't hear anyone come in from the outside door.* When I started for the door, an angel appeared and said to me, "Don't open the door!"

I called out to whoever had rapped on the door, "Who's there?"

A man replied, "We're here for Lisa."

I replied, "There's no Lisa here."

The man said, "This is Apartment Two, isn't it?"

I said, "Yes, but there are apartment number two's in all twenty-five apartment buildings."

The man left, and I immediately went to the window. I watched as two young men went across the playground area and into another building. I found out later they had broken into two more apartments and ransacked them, especially taking jewelry. All I could say was, "Thank You, Jesus, for sending Your angels to protect me!"

Then the angel said to me, "Why are you astonished? I will explain to you the mystery" (Revelation 17:7).

FOOD FOR THOUGHT: What exciting stories of help from angels that these people have experienced. Have you ever wondered, *How is it possible for an angel to appear exactly timed to meet the crisis? Do they have a foreknowledge of events or are they sent by God just at the appropriate time?* The more questions are answered, the more I seem to have. Let's be comforted with the thought that some day all our questions will be answered in the next life.

CHAPTER 17

GRANDMA WAS IN THE CAR!

This story is a different one. Our writer encountered help in a most unusual way.

Saturday started out like any other weekend with our kids' ballgames to attend and grocery shopping to do. I had to work the second shift that night at my job as an operator at the local answering service. I didn't like working second shift very much because it took time away from my kids, but at least this was a weekend and I had my morning with them. My husband, Mark, worked third shift in a department store.

It was a normal workday—not too busy and not too slow. Around 10:00 pm I started to get a splitting headache. My shift was over at midnight, but I decided to leave a little early to go the store for some Tylenol and also see my husband on his break. When I arrived he was busy, so I made my purchase and planned to go straight home to bed. I walked through the parking lot, which was empty except for my car, and started to drive home.

I took the normal way home and was on the bridge when I looked over at the passenger's seat and saw my Grandma Donna sitting there. This was pretty amazing for she wasn't in the car when I left the parking lot, and more importantly, she had died two years earlier! With the sense in my heart that something awful was about to happen, I screamed.

At that very moment I was hit from behind. My SUV flipped over, back to front, and then rolled from side to side. I felt as if I were on a runaway carnival ride. I just knew I was going to die. Thoughts raced through my mind: *What is going to happen to my four kids? How will my husband handle this? My parents are going to be devastated.*

Then as fast as it happened, everything stopped. I was hanging upside down, suspended by my seat belt, and my glasses had flown off my face. The car was upside down and still running. I could see feet next to the window, and I rolled the window down. Two passersby helped pull me out of the car. I wasn't bleeding; I hadn't even been cut or scratched. However, moving around was painful, and when the ambulance came, they put me on a straight board and took me to our local hospital.

I had been hit by a drunk driver. I had some broken ribs and messed up my back, my knee, and my leg. The car was totaled, but none of the window glass had broken. Most importantly, I was alive. I was going to have some problems, but my life had been spared. God had saved my life!

A few hours later the emergency room staff released me because my injuries didn't warrant a hospital stay. When I finally arrived home and fell into bed, I had the most interesting and beautiful dream or vision. I saw myself talking to my husband at the store just as I had done. It was almost a rerun or a backwards deja vu. Next, I saw myself walking out to my car, but this time I also saw other people in the parking lot. I saw my Grandpa Bill who had died a month before I was born. I saw my friend Brandy who had died when we were little kids. I saw my Uncle Tom, who had just died earlier that month, and my daughter's friend, Jeffery, who had died in an accident at the beginning of fourth grade.

I saw other people whom I didn't know. And then I saw Jesus! They all smiled at me as I kept walking to my car. I saw myself get into the car and drive away. I saw the intersection, the turn, and the bridge. I saw my grandmother sitting in the passenger's seat. And then I watched as I was hit. But this time, all those people I had seen in the parking lot—the ones I knew and the ones I didn't—were in the car with me too. They joined hands and made a circle around me, singing, protecting me, and keeping me safe.

I woke up crying, feeling a peace inside me that I had never felt before, and I knew that I was going to be okay. I knew I had been blessed. My life had been spared for a reason, and I consider every day I now live as a gift sent directly from Him!

He said, "Look! I see four men walking around in the fire, unbound and unharmed, and the fourth looks like a son of the gods" (Daniel 3:25).

FOOD FOR THOUGHT: No matter where we are or where we go, God is near. When our lives are miraculously spared, we tend to appreciate them more. I believe that there are many times we are spared and never know it. We need to thank God for every day.

CHAPTER 18

DO YOU BELIEVE IN ANGELS?

*W*alt Shepard now does! Depressed over a broken relationship, he was ready to end his life. In the dark, predawn hours one Sunday, he accelerated his sports car to more than 100 miles per hour on Interstate 10, north of New Orleans.

Ahead, on the side of the road, he saw what appeared to be an abandoned car. Here was his chance. He plowed into the back of the abandoned car. There was an explosion, and then both vehicles burst into flames.

The night manager of a nearby motel heard the crash and called 911. Walt had been thrown through his windshield and was lying on top of the mangled engine, trapped by the crumpled hood. Fire raged all around him, and he lost consciousness.

The highway patrol arrived quickly, but the fire was so intense it kept the officers away from the wreckage. Suddenly both the officers and the motel manager were amazed when they saw two figures approach the car and pull Walt from the flames.

The officers wanted to interview the two strangers to find out more about the accident, but as soon as the man was loaded into an ambulance, they mysteriously disappeared.

His missionary father spoke with those who had witnessed his son's rescue. They all agreed that the two unidentified figures had approached the car as if it had not been on fire. This rescue had completely baffled the highway patrol.

Walt began months of recovery with surgery and therapy. He struggled with anger, but he also began to think about his life and upbringing in the home of Presbyterian missionaries. Lying in a body cast on his hospital bed, frustrated and desperate, he finally decided to pray. He said, "Lord, I can't take it. I need Your forgiveness. Come into my life and clean me up." The next morning he woke up after the best night's rest he could remember having in the previous five years!

That day, his dad came to visit him and was overjoyed to hear about his son's prayer. His dad said, "Son, I think you were saved by two angels so you would have the opportunity to do what you did this week—get your life right with God."

At first Walt was skeptical, but now after some years have passed, he says, "I believe angels are simply part of God's natural dealings with us. It's amazing, but I believe angels rescued me from the fire that morning. And I believe they haven't stopped working."

Do you believe this story? I can't verify it because I wasn't there at this scene. But I can tell you it fits into the biblical context of what angels have done in the past, are doing in today's world, and will be doing in the future.

Are not all angels ministering spirits sent to serve those who will inherit salvation? (Hebrews 1:14).

FOOD FOR THOUGHT: All right, let's consider the question again: Do you really believe in angels? The critics have always expressed themselves by casting doubt on things of the spiritual realm. But you have a better resource than that. The Bible, from beginning to end, simply assumes the very real existence of angels. In fact, the Bible contains more than 300 direct references to angels! Check it out for yourself in your Bible concordance.

CHAPTER 19

HEAVEN'S EMERGENCY SERVICE

While sharing a cup of coffee with a friend, Johnny Spruill said, "You know, I am certainly glad angels don't take coffee breaks or go on vacation or sleep like we humans do. I am glad they are on 24-hour duty."

Johnny is a licensed tanker-man and owns a partnership in a business that specializes in loading and unloading petroleum products from barges in the Port of Houston. As Johnny was working one morning in 1970, the Spirit of the Lord spoke so vividly that he jumped and looked around, thinking someone had spoken to him. The message was this: "Johnny, you shall walk through the valley of the shadow of death. But fear no evil, for I am with you, and My angels have charge over you."

At about ten o'clock that night, Johnny was very busy trying to unload four barges that had come into port earlier that evening. Only one other employee was available to assist him.

A high wind was blowing, and the barges bounced

against one another and crashed and bucked in the waves. Walking on the barges and jumping from one to another was especially difficult but necessary since the unloading hoses had to be moved from barge to barge across these huge vessels.

Suddenly, just as Johnny stepped out to cross over to the next barge, a wave came up, parting the barges. Johnny fell more than twelve feet into the water and went under, deep enough to come up under one of the barges rather than between them. He tried desperately to fight back sickening fear and panic.

Just as he finally was able to surface between the barges, he remembered the strange words spoken to him that morning: "Fear no evil!"

Johnny began to praise the Lord for help and deliverance. On either side of him were these two barges, looming in the darkness for all the world like giant steel coffins. If the wind blew again or another ship passed by in the channel, the barges would come together crushing him. He barely had room to turn sideways in the water between them.

He attempted to place his feet on either barge and climb out, but it was no use! He couldn't get a grip on the slick, wet sides of the barges, and the decks were more than twelve feet straight up. The wind continued blowing and the barges rocked! Johnny's assistant was supposed to be two barges over, working around the pump and wouldn't be able to hear anything above the noise. Johnny called out anyway, and immediately the assistant answered. He threw down a rope ladder, and Johnny quickly climbed out of the dark death trap.

For no reason that he could think of, minutes earlier the

assistant had felt a hand pushing him away from his work station, and he had walked over to where Johnny had been working. During this time when Johnny was between the barges, the barges remained stationary as if there were no wind or waves. The sea around them had suddenly been made calm!

Johnny said, "God's angels were on duty that night. One quieted the waves and one held the barges apart while the other summoned my assistant. We can all be glad our angels don't take coffee breaks!"

> *Last night an angel of the God whose I am and whom I serve stood beside me and said, "Do not be afraid, Paul… and God has graciously given you the lives of all who sail with you." So keep up your courage, men, for I have faith in God that it will happen just as he told me* (Acts 27:23-25).

FOOD FOR THOUGHT: One of the promised blessings of the believer is to enjoy divine protection from accidents. Have you ever thought just how this is to happen? Psalm 91 is explicit concerning this protection from harmful accidents as the above story illustrated. This may bring to mind another question as to why we all aren't protected from disasters all the time. That's for someone wiser than me to answer, but I still take the promise of protection as a 24/7 blessing.

CHAPTER 20

NO ACCIDENT

It would be nice if every story were a pleasant one, but of course since we are human, that can never be.

In the late eighties, John Gordon of Springfield, Missouri, sensed the prompting of the Lord to devote more time to prayer. So, along with several others, a 4:30 a.m. prayer meeting was birthed. That meeting continued for quite a while until people began dropping out or moving away. They found themselves moving from one location to another, with each move bringing fewer people. After about three years of getting up at 4:30 a.m., John began to grow weary. Finally, he made the decision to take a small sabbatical from the meeting. To his friend Ed's credit, Ed warned him: "John, I don't think you should do this." But his mind was made up; he needed a break, and he decided that someone else could carry the ball for awhile.

Let's pick this story up with John's words:

This decision turned into a slide, then a fall, to the point that I became disinterested in the important spiritual things in my life and became more interested in worldly pursuits. I do not want to imply that I was on a big sinning program or something, but I was not interested in what was important to the Lord. I thought I would get back to spiritual things later.

About six months into my new attitude, I was test-driving a small Toyota pickup truck that a friend of mine wanted to sell. The weather that day was rainy and windy. I decided to take the truck out on the four-lane highway to see how it handled, then cut back across the country by Lake Springfield before driving back home. While driving across the dam that day, I can only tell you that what happened was a supernatural experience. It was as though an invisible hand reached down and gave that truck a shove, and off I went into a spin about a 100 feet across the little dam. The truck got almost to the end of the dam when I heard a distinctive voice: "John," He said, "I'd like to talk to you for a minute."

Upon hearing His voice, I remember shouting, "Lord, help me!"

He didn't respond immediately. The truck spun until it fell off an embankment near the end of the dam. The truck was pinned against a tree and held in place with a slim branch about thirty feet above a small cliff; through the side window I could see this limb about one foot from my head. It held the driver's side door shut and was all that was holding the truck from falling over the cliff. I didn't dare move for fear of dislodging or breaking that little branch. I was scared to death that limb would break, causing the truck to flip end over end down to the ravine below. At that moment, the voice spoke clearly: "John, you have taken Me for granted. Come back to Me." The voice did not have to say anything more—I got the message!

Just then, a couple on their way to work saw me pinned against the tree, shouted to make sure I was okay, and then called for a tow truck. I stayed pinned in the truck until it was towed to safety. But I did not soon forget what the Lord had said to me. I sure did not want to ever take Him for granted again.

Praise the Lord, you his angels, you mighty ones who do his bidding, who obey his word... (Psalm 103:20).

FOOD FOR THOUGHT: And there's another moral for us to consider from such a story. Are you attempting to run from God? Have you decided that doing your own thing is more important than being part of God's plan? Perhaps this is the place and time to do some serious thinking about this issue at hand.

CHAPTER 21

THE ANGEL CUSTOMERS

Today Robert owns an over-the-road trucking company, but before he got into the trucking business, he had purchased a sporting goods store. He was the lone employee in the beginning, and the store happened to be in an out-of-the-way part of town, which helped to make him feel even more isolated.

One day while expressing his concerns about his business to his pastor, the idea struck him to ask the pastor and some of the church elders to come over and pray for his protection and that of his store. When they came, they also prayed that anyone who came to purchase a gun for the wrong reasons would not be able to do so.

Sometime later, a very tough, rough looking, tattooed character approached the store. Through the storefront window, Robert saw that this man was accompanied by six or seven other equally tough-looking men on motorcycles parked in front. Immediately Robert sensed that this man did not have good intentions. Standing by the gun counter, the man asked too many odd types of questions, so Robert refused to sell any guns or ammunition to him and told him to leave. The man left in an angry huff, jumped on his bike, and motioned for the others to follow. Once outside, he made an obscene gesture through the window at Robert and pealed out of the parking lot with tires squealing and pipes roaring.

The next morning, this same man returned with his gang plus a few more, but this time he didn't enter the store. The men simply began circling the store in the parking lot on their bikes. This, no doubt, was done with the intent of intimidating Robert or as a prelude to something worse. They kept up this harassment most of the day. They would drive out of the lot and return again in a few minutes to again circle and leave. All the while they would be looking through the front window at Robert.

Alone in the store, Robert prayed, "Lord, help me! Please send your angels to protect me and keep the store safe from harm."

After several hours of this harassment, the leather-jacketed gang drove out of the lot and never returned again.

Later, one of Robert's regular customers dropped by the store to visit. He mentioned that he'd been by earlier in the day but hadn't bothered to come in. Robert asked him why.

"Well, because the inside of your store was packed full of customers. I knew you'd be so busy you wouldn't have time to visit with me, so I just left." Yet...NO ONE was in the store at any time that day, except Robert!

Daniel answered, "O king, live forever! My God sent his angel, and he shut the mouths of the lions. They have not hurt me" (Daniel 6:21).

FOOD FOR THOUGHT: Is this just another story of angelic protection, or is it more than that? How often do we take for granted the fact that God is on our side and concerned about everything that concerns us?

CHAPTER 22

THE GUIDE
FOR THE GUIDE DOG

A blind man named John, living in New York, recently acquired a guide dog named Dustin that had been bred and raised in California. Dustin had proven to be quite a capable guide dog, but he was a newcomer to New England winters and its snow. During his first snowstorm, the dog became disoriented and began to have trouble functioning as they went for a walk outside their Long Island apartment. Let's let John tell his story:

I wasn't doing too well in the snow. No one was out on the street so there were no sounds to steer me. Contrary to what most people think, guide dogs do not find the way for a blind person. The blind person really directs the dog through spoken commands.

After a very harrowing forty-five minutes, Dustin and I finally made it back to our apartment. We were safe for awhile, but guide dogs must be walked regularly, at least twice a day, which meant that later on that day we would have to go out again. I live alone with my dog, so taking him out in the middle of the storm was my responsibility.

Later on that day, I was visiting with a friend on the phone. During this conversation I mentioned something about Dustin having had a difficult time in the snowstorm. My friend offered, "Next time, why don't you ask God to go with you?" So I did.

The time came for our next walk, and trusting that God would be with us, I stepped out with Dustin into the swirling snow. It wasn't long before the snow was stinging our faces, and finding a path through the drifts proved difficult. Dustin whined more than a little. "Okay, boy," I said to him, "the Lord is with us." And then I gave him a command a blind person gives only when another person is leading the way: "Dustin, follow!"

I sensed Dustin perk up and immediately he took off just as if he were following someone as I had commanded. We proceeded much more easily on our walk and then headed back to our apartment.

A young woman I know who lives in our building came up to us and offered to walk with us to the main entrance. Then she said, "We'll just follow the footprints—yours and the dog's and that other person's."

How about that? Even a blind person can have an angelic encounter! Why not? Could it have been that the dog really saw the angel or just followed the tracks in the snow? Did the dog see the angel, but the kind young lady did not?

Every angel story is a fabulous experience. I marvel at the variety of the ways in which these take place and the interaction between us and them. Here it seems a guide dog saw the angel. This shouldn't be hard to believe because the Bible talks about a donkey that saw an angel when his master didn't.

Balaam got up in the morning, saddled his donkey and went with the princes of Moab. But God was very angry when he went and the angel of the Lord stood in the road to oppose. Balaam was riding on his donkey, and his two servants were with him. When the donkey saw the angel of the Lord standing in the road with a drawn sword in his hand, she turned off the road into a field. Balaam beat her to get her back on the road (Numbers 22:21-23).

FOOD FOR THOUGHT: What fabulous stories! A dog follows an angel in a snowstorm, and a donkey sees an angel with a drawn sword! In each case, the humans didn't see the angel, but the animals did. You need to take the time to read the entire donkey and Balaam story (Numbers 22:21-35). Three times the donkey saw the angel and stopped, and each time she was beaten. Finally the eyes of her owner were opened and he said, "I have sinned" because he beat the donkey three times. The angel didn't approve of the beatings. Can you assume that angels treat animals kindly too? Read the rest of the story in the book of Numbers and find out!

CHAPTER 23

COULD IT HAVE BEEN?

In September of 1939, Hitler and his army invaded Poland and in a matter of days conquered it at the beginning of World War II. Leaving Poland in ruins, the huge army of Germany moved west. The world looked on in wonder and horror. It was thought that France, with one of the largest standing armies in the world (an army of some six million soldiers) would be able to defend itself. But in ten short months, Germany had marched across France and Europe. This demoralized the Allied armies, essentially breaking the back of their resistance.

A discouraged and battered Allied army stood on the banks of the English Channel at Dunkirk, France, waiting for the British to evacuate them. It was a miracle that the English were able to withdraw as many troops as they did. They used anything available that floated to bring back as many soldiers as possible. This defeat meant much of the Allies' equipment was left behind or destroyed by the conquering Germans. England became the last stronghold of freedom in that part of the world. It looked as though Hitler would succeed in his plan to conquer Europe!

The Allied troops had no sooner safely reached British soil when Hitler called a surprise meeting of his generals, some of the best military minds in the world. He asked them to make a decision as to whether or not to invade England or wait for a more opportune time. When would there have been a better time? Hitler had the demoralized Allied army in his hip pocket on the verge of total defeat!

Although he knew Great Britain would offer stiff resistance, Hitler thought he would be able to overcome them in a matter of months. According to conventional wisdom, there really wasn't a decision to be made.

Now here's where this story gets interesting. According to Hilton Sutton, who served in our Air Force during these events, a number of divine interventions occurred, including the following incident.

At the surprise meeting Hitler had arranged, a strange "general"—not a German and not a man previously known to Hitler's staff—also made an appearance. This strange general persuaded Hitler and his staff not to invade England but to wait until the German army was stronger and victory was assured. It was decided the German army would invade Russia rather than England!

Had Hitler invaded England, conquered it, and then moved eastward to invade Russia, the outcome of WWII could have been much different. Because Hitler and his staff of military geniuses listened to this strange general, Germany plunged into Russia ill prepared and overconfident.

General Rommel, the German "desert fox," had General Montgomery and his army on the run in North Africa. His troops were poised and ready to strike the final blow to Monty's army when Hitler again called a surprise meeting of his generals. Once more, this same strange visiting general convinced them to recall Rommel to Germany and replace him with another general, who was not prepared for desert warfare. This allowed Monty to recover and launch a counterattack, resulting in a major English victory. Then the Americans came on the scene, and Germany was in retreat.

One more time, Hitler called a staff meeting to make a major decision—whether to produce jet aircraft or continue hurling bombs at Great Britain. Again a strange visiting general was present and convinced Hitler and his staff not to take the time to set up an assembly line to produce jet aircraft. By the time the Germans realized their mistake in not mass-producing jet planes, the United States had gained total air supremacy and was able to destroy most of the German industry.

Who in the world was this visiting general who continued to influence Hitler and his brilliant staff? It's believed, according to Hilton Sutton, that nobody in the world could have pulled off such a daring feat other than an angel! It could have been none other than "Michael," the Chief of Staff of the warring armies of heaven!

Hard to believe? Wait a minute!

At that time Michael, the great prince who protects your people will arise. There will be a time of distress such as has not happened from the beginning of nations until then. But at that time your people—everyone whose name is found written in the book—will be delivered (Daniel 12:1).

FOOD FOR THOUGHT: The archangel Michael is associated with war throughout the Bible. In Revelation 12, John writes that Michael and his angels will make war against Satan and his angels. Note the term "archangel" or "high angel" is specifically applied to Michael. Then there is the story in 2 Kings 19:14-19 when King Hezekiah was threatened by the Assyrians, and God sent His angel through the enemy camp and destroyed 185,000 enemy soldiers! God's special agents were on duty back there in history, why not in our modern world? You decide—was the strange visiting general an angel or possibly even Michael the archangel?

CHAPTER 24

THE ANGELS OF MONS

*A*ccording to this report in the London Evening News, Arthur Machen told how the tiny British expeditionary force, outnumbered three to one, was apparently saved by heavenly reinforcements.

The "angels of Mons" and the accounts of their numbers have varied from one platoon to another as to how they suddenly took up a position between the British and the Germans. Understandably, the enemy fell back in confusion. Historically, a great deal of controversy surrounds the events of this story.

This battle took place on August 26, 1914, and when this story appeared in Allied newspapers in September, most of the survivors were still stationed in France. According to one account, a British officer said that while his army was in retreat from Mons, a unit of German cavalry came charging after them. The British ran for a place from which to make a last stand, but the Germans got there first. Expecting almost certain death, the British troops turned and saw, to their astonishment, a troop of angels between them and the enemy.

The German horses were terrified at what was taking place and stampeded in all directions.

Later, a British army chaplain, the Rev. C.M. Chavasse, recorded that he had heard similar accounts of the miraculous Mons angelic deliverance from a brigadier general and two of his officers. A lieutenant colonel also described how he, too, during this retreat watched as his battalion was escorted for about twenty minutes by a host of phantom cavalry.

From the German side came a confirming account that their men refused to charge a certain point where the British line was broken because of the presence of a very large number of troops. According to the Allied records of this battle, not a single British soldier was in the immediate area.

This is one of those historical stories having many versions, some denials and few plausible explanations. About the only thing we know is that something miraculous and unusual intervened in this battle of August 26, 1914.

This particular story has been around for a long time and is one of those that is still very controversial. What is quite noteworthy about these accounts is that not one of them is reported firsthand. In each case officers and soldiers wished to remain anonymous because their disclosure might hinder any future promotions they were in line to receive. In other words, no one bragged about it to gain any fame whatsoever.

So we can continue with speculation about the reality of what really happened. One of the things of interest to me is that none of the officers or soldiers involved wanted to be identified with the story because it might have an effect on how they would be perceived. I've also found this to be the case in many stories of angel encounters today. Many people have volunteered their stories with this reservation: "I have had this experience but have never told anybody because they might think I'm nuts." But they have shared the details with me apparently because they perceive me as someone who will not ridicule them. This is one of the reasons I have changed the names in many of the stories or in other ways disguised the identity of the people.

> *God is a righteous judge, a God who expresses his wrath every day. If he does not relent, he will sharpen his sword; he will bend and string his bow. He has prepared his deadly weapons; he makes ready his flaming arrows*
> (Psalm 7:11-13)

FOOD FOR THOUGHT: Think with me about the military aspect of angels. Clearly a large part of their work is warfare. Why? Because God is a warrior God. "The Lord is a warrior; the Lord is his name" (Exodus 15:3). Yes, God is a warrior and He wins every battle! Therefore, when angels engage in warfare, they never lose either! And we can be most thankful that God is a warrior, and He commands warrior angels.

CHAPTER 25

I CAN FACE IT UNAFRAID!

A number of years ago when we lived in Madison, Wisconsin, my wife, Donna, and I were privileged to travel to Milwaukee where we were part of a crowd that heard the late Corrie Ten Boom. It took place in a theater, and we were seated about mid-way back in the middle section. This is the story as I remember her telling it.

Together, Betsie (my sister) and I, along with the other women, were herded into a most terrifying building. It took place in the Nazi Ravensbruck prison camp. At the first table were women who took all our possessions. Everyone had to undress completely and then went into another room where our hair was checked.

I asked a woman who was busy checking the possessions of the new arrivals if I might use the toilet. She pointed to a door, and I discovered the toilet was just a hole in the shower room floor. Betsie was with me all this time.

Suddenly I had a thought. "Quick, take off your woolen underwear," I whispered to her. I rolled it up with mine and laid the bundle in a corner along with my little Bible. The spot was alive with cockroaches, but I didn't worry about that. I felt strangely alive, relieved, and happy. "The Lord is answering our prayers, Betsie," I whispered. "We shall not have to make the sacrifice of all our clothes."

We then hurried back to the line of women waiting to be undressed. Later, after we had our delousing showers and put on our shirts and shabby dresses, I hid the roll of underwear and my Bible under my dress. Obviously it did bulge out, but I prayed, "Lord, cause now your angels to surround me; and let them not be transparent today because the guards must not see me."

I felt perfectly at ease. Calmly I passed the guards. Everybody was being checked on all four sides, front and back and sides. Not a single bulge under the clothes escaped the eyes of the guards. The woman in front of me had attempted to hide a warm woolen vest under her dress, but it was taken from her. They let me pass because they didn't see me. Betsie, behind me, was searched.

But it wasn't over yet. Outside we had another search, with more danger. On each side of the doorway were women who looked us over once more. This time they felt over the body of each one who passed. It was another thorough search.

I just knew they couldn't see me. I was calm. I knew the angels were still surrounding me. So I wasn't surprised when they passed me through. They searched the woman in front of me and Betsie in back of me, but they didn't see me and so I passed through this search too. Inside of me rose up a jubilant cry of victory and deliverance, "O Lord, if Thou dost so answer my prayer, I can face even Ravensbruck unafraid!"

And she did! Her story is fabulous and faith building. I would encourage you, if you haven't already read it, to get her story in book form. You will be fascinated. It's a story of true deliverance.

For it seems to me that God has put us apostles on display at the end of the procession, like men condemned in the arena. We have been made a spectacle to the whole universe, to angels as well as to men (1 Corinthians 4:9).

FOOD FOR THOUGHT: Obviously angels are watching our journey. The events of our lives are of importance because angels are interested spectators.

CHAPTER 26

THE BOOKSTORE ANGEL

*R*uth Graham (the late wife of evangelist Billy Graham) related this strange happening which took place in a Christian bookstore in Shanghai, China, in 1942. Her father, Dr. L. Nelson Bell, who served in the hospital in Tsingkiangpu, Kiangsu province, told the story.

The setting was the bookstore in which Dr. Bell bought his gospel portions and tracts to distribute among his patients. After the Japanese had taken control of much of China, they imposed their control on the Chinese. One morning, about nine o'clock, a Japanese truck stopped outside the bookstore. It was carrying five Japanese marines, and the truck was half-filled with books. The bookstore assistant, who happened to be alone in the store at this time, realized with dismay that they had come to confiscate his stock.

Jumping from the truck, the marines made for the bookstore door. Before they could enter, a neatly dressed Chinese gentleman came into the store ahead of them.

The shop assistant knew practically everybody who frequented the store, but he did not know this stranger! For some unknown reason, the marines seemed unable to follow him into the store. They stood outside and milled around, looking in at the four large storefront windows. No one else was in the store and no one else outside, yet each time they attempted to enter the store they were unable to do so.

For a bit more than two hours they stood around, looking in but never setting foot inside. The well-dressed stranger asked what the soldiers wanted, and the assistant shopkeeper explained the Japanese had taken books from the other book-shops in the area and now wanted to take some from his bookstore.

The two prayed together and this stranger encouraged him, and so more than two hours passed. It was as though some kind of barrier had been placed across the entrance blocking their entry. At last the marines shook their heads, climbed back into their truck and drove away.

Then the stranger also left. He had spent more than two hours in the store without making a single purchase. He had not even made an inquiry about any of the items in the store.

Later the same day, the bookstore owner, Mr. Christopher Willis (whose Chinese name was Lee), returned. The shop assistant asked him, Mr. Lee, do you believe in angels?"

"I do," replied Mr. Lee.

"So do I, Mr. Lee," said the assistant who then told the storeowner the events of the morning.

Could this stranger have been one of God's protecting angels? Dr. Nelson Bell always thought so.

How about you? Do you believe in angels? It's quite likely you do or you would not be reading this book. Or maybe you are a person who is searching for answers, and you're looking for evidence that angels might be real. Believers accept the

truth about angels by faith based on the teachings of God's
Word.

*The angel of the Lord found Hagar near a spring in the
desert; it was the spring that is beside the road to Shur*
(Genesis 16:7).

FOOD FOR THOUGHT: Would the enemies, who
attack Christians, be thwarted more if we grasped the concept that God's angels are on duty nearby to help in time of
need? It's an interesting idea to ponder.

CHAPTER 27

THE ANGEL TRUCK DRIVER

The following story was related to me but the circumstances, names, and location have been changed.

It happened in a small town and a church in a farming area in a midwestern state. Pastor Vernon Anderson was a good leader, considered to be the pastor of the entire community, and was a wonderful man. His church was thriving and growing, and he used a number of lay people to assist in many ways. Among these volunteers was a man who was the worship leader and was well-known in the congregation and the community. Sometimes difficult things happen. This worship leader was discovered to be having an extra-marital affair with another woman. When this sin was uncovered, the pastor immediately dismissed him from his duties of leading the congregation in worship.

The man reacted in anger when informed, and among some of the things he said to the pastor was this statement: "I'll get you for this if it's the last thing I do!" After this declaration, he stomped out of the pastor's office and slammed the door.

The next day, the pastor was driving out of the church parking lot in his pickup and was stopped by this irate man named Tom. As the man approached the truck, Pastor Anderson reached across the seat and took his heavy framing hammer from the tool box and held it in his lap, just in case. Tom threatened him again but did him no harm, just verbally venting his anger at the pastor for making him an example and accusing him of exposing his affair for the whole town to see.

Later the next day, Pastor Anderson received a phone call from Tom. This time Tom seemed calm and asked if he could meet the pastor to offer an apology for his behavior. The pastor agreed, and Tom named the place. They were to meet on the top of a hill on a gravel road about four miles out of town. The pastor really didn't think too much about the location but was grateful for the opportunity to make things right between them.

At the appointed time, the pastor drove out of town on the gravel road and stopped on the hilltop where they were supposed to meet. He got out of his pickup to wait for Tom and soon saw the dust cloud behind Tom's truck, coming fast in his direction. Tom slammed on his brakes and skidded to a stop behind the pastor's pickup. At almost the same time and from the opposite direction came a brand new, red Chevrolet water truck that pulled to the side of the road, opposite the pastor and Tom.

Tom took one look at the red truck, jumped into his own truck, spun it around, and spewed gravel in all directions as he beat a track back in the direction from which he had come. The pastor watched him disappear into the distance and turned to talk with the driver of the water truck, but both it and the driver had disappeared. He could see a couple of miles in both directions from the top of the hill and there was no tank truck or driver to be seen!

Later, when the pastor asked the man who delivered water in their town if he had purchased a new truck, he was told that the man still drove his old one.

A few days later, the pastor received another call from Tom who asked, "Why did you have that other truck come when I was to meet you?"

Pastor Anderson replied, "I don't know who it was or where it came from. He just drove up."

Tom continued, "I wanted to meet you on that hill because nobody is ever around there, and I planned to kill you."

Yes, Tom did eventually apologize and asked forgiveness. He repented and became a part of church life again. The pastor, to this day, hopes to see the red water tank truck once more. He told me that because of the rural setting he can recognize everybody's vehicle in quite a large area, but no one ever had a red truck with a stainless steel tank!

And Elisha prayed, "O Lord, open his eyes so that he may see." Then the Lord opened the servant's eyes, and he looked and saw the hills full of horses and chariots of fire all round Elisha (2 Kings 6:17).

FOOD FOR THOUGHT: Jean Paul Richter said, "The guardian angels of life sometimes fly so high as to be beyond our sight, but they are always looking down upon us." How many times have you been delivered from danger and have not even been aware of your angelic protection?

SECTION 3

CHILDREN

Just for Kids
Angels

See that you do not look down on one of these little ones.
For I tell you that their angels in heaven always see
the face of my Father in heaven (Matthew 18:10).

CHAPTER 28

FIRST INTO THE FIELD

$\mathcal{I}$t was springtime on this family's fifteen hundred acre farm in North Dakota, and the oldest son, age fourteen, whom we'll call Eugene, was anxious to be the first farmer into the field in that area. Bragging rights were at stake. On this particular day, school was out, and Eugene had begged his dad to let him be the first farmer out in the field. He argued that it was dry enough. Finally his dad relented and said, "Okay, take the D-Case (which is a four-plow tractor) and the disc, and do the back eighty. But be careful."

Eugene was one happy young man! He plowed until it was time to quit and then unhitched the disc and started out for home on the tractor. He was standing up because the tractor had a hand clutch and was easier to drive in that position. He was going at a wide open speed when he hit a furrow in the field. The tractor lurched and he was thrown off!

He flew over the steering wheel and landed in front of the right rear wheel and attempted to get away, but the lugs on the tire caught his head and ran over it, mashing it into the newly turned earth. He was stunned but managed to get to his feet and run the quarter mile to the farm house, shouting as he banged open the door, "I've been run over by the tractor!"

His parents quickly got him into the car and sped toward town and the nearest hospital. The emergency room doctor took a quick look and asked what had happened. Eugene said, "I've been run over by the tractor." The doctor looked again and said, "No, you haven't."

But Eugene insisted and his parents backed him up. The doctor finally relented and took an x-ray. It showed multiple fractures of his skull and face. Then the doctor admitted him to a room, and the swelling began. Soon his head was bloated to about twice the normal size. The doctor then told the parents there was no chance Eugene would survive such injuries.

The pastor and their church were alerted, and everyone began to pray for Eugene. By the next evening, family members were assembled to say their last farewell to a dying son and brother. His head and face had turned black, his vital signs were slowing down, and he passed into a coma. The family members were all there along with the pastor of their church. It was a solemn time as they prayed and waited. The doctors again assured the family that Eugene could not survive the night. He had been placed inside an oxygen tent to help with the breathing.

Suddenly Eugene sat up in the tent! He asked what day it was. Stunned, they replied, "March 29."

Eugene asked, "Why are all of you here?"

"Because we were told you were going to die tonight."

"That's funny; I feel great! I'm ready to go home and help you in the fields," he replied to his dad.

"How come you are feeling so great?" asked another, not able to understand what was happening.

Eugene smiled through his swollen face, "Can't you see? There's an angel sitting on my bed, and he told me everything will be all right!" Nobody else in the room saw the angel, but the healing took place right before their eyes!

Eugene was completely healed with no complications and is alive and well today!

Are not all angels ministering spirits sent to serve those who will inherit salvation? (Hebrews 1:14)

FOOD FOR THOUGHT: Do angels have the power to heal someone? No! The power to heal comes from Jesus Christ and His sacrifice on Calvary, as it says "by His stripes we are healed." However angels can well be the messengers of healing by carrying the good news that healing is taking place. Remember, angels are not the source of healing; God is!

CHAPTER 29

MIRACLE UNDER THE HOOD

The origins of a story often cannot be traced. The following one, which was told to a nationwide TV audience by the late Howard Conatser, founder of the Beverly Hills Baptist Church of Dallas, Texas, is one of those stories.

I do not recall their names, so we'll call these two teenage sisters Karen and Susan. They had been shopping in a suburban mall, and when they were ready to leave, they were chagrined to find that it was already dark outside. Their father had told them to come home before dark. From the mall exit they saw their car, the only one left in that particular section of the parking lot.

They were nervous and hesitant to go out the door. They stood waiting, hoping some other customers would come along so they could all walk out together. The girls were aware of the current crime wave in area shopping malls and remembered their dad's final warning as they left the house: "Don't stay too late!"

"Let's get with it…now!" Susan shifted her packages,

pushed open the door, and walked as fast as she could with Karen following. Both were looking from side to side as they quickly made their way to the car. Karen shoved the key into the door lock, hastily got in, and reached across to open Susan's door when they both heard the sound of running feet coming towards them from behind. They turned to look and panicked because racing toward their car were two ominous looking men!

One of the men shouted, "We got you! You're not going anywhere!"

Susan jumped in and both locked their doors just in time. With shaking hands, Karen turned the ignition switch. Nothing happened! She tried again and again—still nothing! Not even a click! They looked at each other with the sinking knowledge that they had no power. The men approached with tire irons in hand, ready to smash a window.

The girls knew they had but scant seconds of safety left, so they grabbed each other's hands and prayed! "Dear God," Susan pleaded, "give us a miracle in the name of Jesus!"

Again Karen turned the key, and the engine roared to life! They raced out of the parking lot, squealing their tires and leaving their astonished would-be attackers behind.

The girls cried all the way home, shocked but relieved. They screeched into the driveway, pulled the car into the garage, burst into the house, and spilled out their story in quick gasps. Their parents held them close and comforted their frightened daughters.

"You're safe, thank God! That's the main thing. But don't do it again," Dad said. Then their father frowned, "It's strange. That car has never failed to start. I'll just take a look at it now."

In the garage he raised the hood, and in one stunned glance, he realized who had brought his daughters home safely that night because no battery was in the car!

The men were amazed and asked, "What kind of man is this? Even the winds and the waves obey him!" (Matthew 8:27)

FOOD FOR THOUGHT: Angels have carried out all kinds of assignments recorded in the Bible—from guarding the entrance to the garden of Eden, feeding Elijah, healing Isaiah's lips, freeing Peter from prison, to guiding John around the New Jerusalem. Protection and deliverance seem to be regular types of assignments for them. Now the question is, has God assigned one particular angel to take care of just you? Lots of folks think that all of us have guardian angels. Only God knows for sure.

CHAPTER 30

ANGELIC PROVISION

*J*onathan remembers well his angelic encounter even though it happened more than seventy years ago. He was ten years old, and the Depression of the thirties was at its peak. He had younger brothers and sisters, and keeping food on the table for the family was one horrendous struggle.

Being the oldest child, one chore assigned to Jonathan was to do the shopping for his mother every Saturday. He would hand the list to the grocer who would help pick out the items on the list. With money in such short supply, this was a highly trusted job for such a small boy, but he did it with pride and a strong sense of responsibility.

On this particular Saturday morning, his mother gave him the grocery list and tucked $10 into his jacket pocket and sent him on his way. She always warned him never to buy anything that was not on the list. When the proprietor had loaded his wagon with the groceries from the list, he stopped at the counter to pay the lady at the cash register. She asked him for $9.74. When he reached into his jacket pocket, the money was gone! Frantic, he searched through every pocket, in his pants, through the jacket again, but no money! He pulled off his shoes and socks, thinking it might be there. He looked under his cap and ran back through the store hoping to see it on the floor. No money! The grocer went through his jacket pockets. Nothing! He began to cry. There was nothing to do but leave the groceries and go home to tell his mother.

Of course, she was angry and upset. To lose $10 in those days was a near catastrophe. They would have nothing to eat that week beyond what had been left in the cupboards—a bleak prospect.

Having done everything he could to find the money, Jonathan crept into the basement to cry. Even though he was only ten, he knew the consequences of what happened. As he was sobbing, he heard a strong, positive, and kind voice coming from behind him. The voice called him by name, "Jonathan, just look in your jacket pocket."

How strange, he thought. He'd been through the jacket at least three times, the clerk at the grocery store had looked in it, and his mother had done the same thing a number of times. Thinking it was foolish to try, nevertheless he stuck his hand into the pocket to feel for the money once more and to satisfy the voice. And there, inside the pocket, he found the wadded up bills—$10 in all!

To this day, more than seventy years later, whenever discouragement strikes, Jonathan still remembers the time in the basement when God heard the cries of a little boy and sent a messenger to put $10 into an empty jacket pocket!

I never get tired of listening to or recounting angel stories. Each is different and unique, but all show the goodness of a loving God to His children when in need. What encouragement and hope they bring!

However, as it is written: "No eye has seen, no ear has heard, no mind has conceived what God has prepared for those who love him" (1 Corinthians 2:9).

FOOD FOR THOUGHT: Have you ever questioned, "Why study or read about angels? What's in it for me?" We need to understand by faith that they may be watching over us, ready to come to our rescue and serve the Lord as they serve us. The realization of this truth is more than comforting, it will assist us in living out a life that gives praise to God.

CHAPTER 31

UNEXPECTED ANGELS

*J*ason Moore shares a story of his encounter with angels when he was just fifteen.

My angels aren't anything like I had expected them to look. The day I turned fifteen was a beautiful, warm, wonderful day in California. My family and I were at the annual church choir picnic when I started not to feel good, and so my dad dropped me back at our house.

While resting in an easy chair, I was also talking on the phone when it suddenly went dead. I tried to get another dial tone, but there was no response. I thought it a bit strange but quickly forgot about it when I smelled smoke. My first thought was that my mom must have left something on the stove or in the oven, so I went to investigate.

I couldn't find anything, and then the smoke detector alarm went off. Not wanting to listen to its piercing noise, I grabbed a towel and began to fan the detector. Well, it took me a few minutes, but finally a light bulb went off in my head that said something might really be wrong, so I ran outside.

As soon as I opened the front door, I saw three large African-American men running towards my house. Startled, I stopped to hear them yelling, "Your house is on fire! Your house is on fire!" I looked back from the front yard, and I could see smoke coming from the top of my house.

There I was fifteen years old and alone with a house fire. I thought, *I have to get the stereo out of the house!* I began to yank our belongings out of the house as fast as I could. All the while, these three big guys were in my house helping me. One ran across the street to call the fire department. Another began hooking up the garden hoses to slow the fire down and keep it from spreading to the houses next door. We were alone for more than five minutes before the fire department arrived. In that time, all our belongings had been safely removed from the house.

When the firemen came, I turned to thank those three guys for their help, but they were gone! I asked my neighbors if they knew where those guys had gone, but no one had seen them at all except me. Where they came from and where they went, I have no idea. Our house sustained a minimum of smoke and water damage because of the help of those three guys. Nothing was lost.

I needed help, direction, and wisdom, which those three offered. They did not stick around for interviews or thanks; they were just there when they were needed. So I really think that the angels the Lord has watching over me are those three big black guys. And since that time, I sure sleep better with that knowledge!

When you pass through the waters, I will be with you; and when you pass through the rivers, they will not sweep over you. When you walk through the fire, you will not be burned; the flames will not set you ablaze. For I am the Lord, your God (Isaiah 43:2-3).

FOOD FOR THOUGHT: What a comfort! Angels are concerned about teenagers too! This may be a special message for all parents who might worry about their teens. So if and when your angels appear, what form do you think they'll take? Will you be able to recognize your angel when it appears?

CHAPTER 32

THE MUD PUDDLE LANDING

oward County, Indiana, Sheriff Jerry Marr received a very disturbing call one Saturday afternoon. His six-year-old grandson, Mikey, had been hit by a car while out fishing with his dad. The father and son were near a bridge by the Kokomo River Reservoir when a woman lost control of her car, slid off the embankment, and hit Mikey at about fifty miles per hour! Sheriff Marr had seen the results of such accidents and feared the worst. When he arrived at St. Joseph Hospital, he rushed to the emergency room to find Mikey conscious and in fairly good spirits.

"Mikey, what happened?" the sheriff asked.

"Well, Pawpaw," replied Mikey, "I was fishin' with Dad and some lady runned me over; I flew into a mud puddle and broke my fishin' pole, and I didn't get to catch no fish!"

As it turned out, the impact propelled Mikey about 200 feet, over a few low level trees and an embankment and into the middle of a mud puddle. His only injuries were to his right femur bone, which had broken in two places. Mikey had to have surgery to place pins in his leg; otherwise he was fine for the experience.

Since all he could talk about was his broken fishing pole, the sheriff went to the store and bought Mikey a new one while he was in surgery so he could have it when he came out.

The next day the sheriff sat with Mikey to keep him company in the hospital room. Mikey was enjoying his new fishing pole and talking about when he could go fishing again. When they were alone, Mikey matter-of-factly said, "Pawpaw, did you know Jesus is real?"

"Well," the sheriff replied, a bit startled. "Yes, Jesus is real to all who believe in Him and love Him in their hearts."

"No," said Mikey. "I mean Jesus is *really* real!"

"What do you mean?" asked the grandfather.

"I know He's real 'cause I saw Him," said Mikey, casting a practice lure into the trash can.

"You did?" asked the sheriff.

"Yep," replied Mikey. "When that lady runned me over and broke my fishing pole, Jesus caught me in His arms and laid me down in the mud puddle."[1]

Daniel answered, "...My God sent his angel, and he shut the mouths of the lions. They have not hurt me, because I was found innocent in his sight..." (Daniel 6:21-22).

FOOD FOR THOUGHT: John Calvin wrote: "The angels are the dispensers and administrators of the divine beneficence toward us; they regard our safety, undertake our defense, direct our ways, and exercise a constant solicitude that no evil befall us." Now...did Mikey actually see Jesus or one of His angels? Interesting, isn't it? No matter, Mikey was spared by some miraculous intervention.

1 *Uniting Men & Meaning,* the magazine of United Methodist Men, Vol. 5, #3, 2002

CHAPTER 33

THE FIRE FIGHTING ANGEL

*A*s a young boy, Jimmy lived in a large old farm house located in rural North Dakota with his mother, father, and five younger brothers and sisters. Making a trip to town to get supplies or groceries would take all day. This incident occurred years before electricity was available to these rural farm people.

One day, Jimmy's parents had to go to another town on business and because of the distance they would have to stay overnight. Because Jimmy was the oldest, he was put in charge of the children. The younger ones were told that they must obey him because he was the head of the family in the absence of Mom and Dad.

The day went pretty well with Jimmy in charge. They all managed to do their assigned chores and had no major problems.

Some good-natured wrestling and horseplay was going on when Jimmy looked across the room at his three-year-old brother and watched to his horror that Benjamin was playing with a lighted candle. He was putting unlit matches into the flame and watching with great glee as they burst into flame. Before Jimmy could reach him, the candle tipped over and fire began to spread on the rug and the bedclothes.

No one could explain what happened next, but in the middle of the confusion and spreading fire, the children looked over at the bedroom door and saw a tall, beautiful being standing in the doorway, which they later decided had to have been an angel. As they watched, the angel blew out the fire and turned and left. The children ran down the hall after the angel and downstairs and outside, but he had just disappeared.

Today, these brothers and sisters are all married, and they have children and grandchildren of their own. But when they have family get-togethers during the holidays, sooner or later the conversation turns to the time they watched an angel blow out the fire on a cold winter's night on a farm in northern North Dakota!

> *For he will command his angels concerning you to guard you in all your ways; they will lift you up in their hands, so that you will not strike your foot against a stone* (Psalm 91:11-12).

FOOD FOR THOUGHT: God sends angels to His children to bring us protection under difficult circumstances. How often have you had angelic protection and didn't even know it was happening?

CHAPTER 34

THE HORSEFLY

The following story was sent to me a few years ago by a nine-year-old boy named Ryan.

My name is Ryan. In August my brother Michael and I were out with my mom when she went up behind our horse named Favor without letting the horse know she was there. Then a horsefly landed on it, and Favor kicked at the bug. She didn't mean to kick Mom in the face. When Mom fell down, I ran toward the house, and all the time I was praying.

I looked back and saw Favor running around, and then I saw the angel. It was huge and had big, big wings and was wearing sandals. It was filled with light and stood over my mom while Favor was galloping around. The angel was standing over Mom so Favor wouldn't run over her.

When I got to the house I called 911, and then Mom came inside. She talked a little and then the ambulance came and took her to the hospital. I'm glad that the angel was there to help her. Lots of people started praying for Mom, and I'm glad God let my mom live.

In my files I have Ryan's handwritten note which obviously had been meticulously written with pencil. I also have his drawing of the huge angel he saw. It's complete with wings and sandals on the feet just like the description he wrote. The angel is colored a bright yellow. I'd say Ryan did a wonderful job in sharing his experience with us and was quite accurate in his angelic reproduction. Yes, his mom survived and is doing well.

See that you do not look down on one of these little ones. For I tell you that their angels in heaven always see the face of my Father in heaven (Matthew 18:10).

FOOD FOR THOUGHT: Do you think the horse named Favor saw the angel just as Ryan did? Remember a donkey was able to see an angel even when his rider Balaam the wayward prophet in the Bible did not see it. For sure, Favor didn't run into or over Mom, according to Ryan. The story Ryan told us is without a doubt a true one. Yes, I know kids have big imaginations, but how many kids see angels? Probably more than we know, so the next time a child tells you or me an angel story, I intend to be a believer! How about you?

CHAPTER 35

A SHOCKING TIME AT THE BOARDING SCHOOL

In the following story, Henrietta W. Romman shares an incredible incident that happened when she was eleven years old in her home town of Khartoum in Africa.

My mom, Juliette, was extremely ill with asthma, which had already affected her heart. It became necessary for her to travel to Egypt for essential treatment, but my parents weren't sure what to do with us five children during that time.

The only solution they could arrive at was that my two younger sisters would go with them, while my two brothers and I would remain safely in Khartoum as boarders in our familiar school premises. Henry and Charles were to stay in the boarding house of the Comboni Catholic School for boys while I was to stay in the same school's boarding house for girls, which was located in the adjoining building.

Our parents left and I began my temporary living arrangements among twenty-five other girls—some were my age and a few were older. Although this took place during the summer vacation, we were still supervised by our school teacher nuns. We enjoyed a wonderful time of play, completing interesting projects, and just being children in the playground. We felt safe and secure under the watchful eyes of the friendly and loving nuns.

As the newcomer, I was privileged to use the separate, beautiful guest bathroom. This particular building was rarely used, so the electrical system had not been checked recently.

Being eleven years old, I felt joyful and highly favored. On the first afternoon at shower time, I entered the bathroom with the necessary change of clothing. After I had showered, I proceeded to dry myself and my hair with a thin towel until the poor thing was soaking wet.

Upon leaving, I proceeded to turn off the lights. I made a half turn with the wet towel between my right hand forefinger and thumb, and reached for the light switch with the same hand. Unfortunately, I didn't just flick the switch but held it and slowly turned it.

What happened next was totally unexpected! My hand stuck to the light switch, and electrical shocks ran through my body with such intensity that I began to shake and scream: "Ah...Ahh...A...A...A...Ah! A...A... A...Ahhh!

All my energy and life quickly drained from my body. I knew I would soon die, and no one would know about it for hours. My mind went blank. I couldn't let loose and continued to shake and moan.

Instantly, out of nowhere, the tall and graceful Sister Maria Questanca, my previous year's teacher, drifted into the room so quietly, grabbed me around the waist, and quickly snatched me away from the light switch. Sorella Maria, as we girls called her, gently carried me over to a nearby chair.

When I thanked my rescuer, she never said a word but simply checked me over to make sure I was all right and then left. I felt so safe and relaxed that I closed my eyes and dozed off to sleep.

Later some girls came and roused me for supper. When I described to them what had just taken place in the bathroom, they were astounded. I told them of the nun's role in saving my life.

"Girls," I shared, "I never knew she was so beautiful, and so kind and so quiet!"

At these words, my friends looked at each other perplexed, and I heard one of them exclaim, "But she is in Italy to visit the Pope!" Another girl asked, "Do you think the electricity spoiled her mind?" One other girl added, "She is imagining strange things."

At their words, I asked, "If this was not the real nun who helped me, then who was she?"

If you make the Most High your dwelling—even the Lord, who is my refuge—then no harm will befall you, no disaster will come near your tent. For He will command His angels concerning you to guard you in all your ways; they will lift you up in their hands, so that you will not strike your foot against a stone. You will tread upon the lion and the cobra; you will trample the great lion and the serpent (Psalm 91:9-13).

FOOD FOR THOUGHT: One of the ministries of angels is to provide protection over believers and children. The above biblical passage is an example of the fulfillment of a promise of angelic protection to us as God's people.

CHAPTER 36

THE BUS RIDING ANGEL

*F*rom North Mankato, Minnesota: Two things are always in short supply when you are a college student: sleep and money with which to travel home. Margarete was away at college, a hardworking, diligent sophomore. She was a resident of a dorm where sleep was in short commodity. Girls being girls, and studies being studies, and boys being subjects of many late night conversations, the nights seemed pretty short.

The Christmas holidays were soon approaching, which meant a trip home was almost in sight. But as always, college professors haven't much heart and usually schedule tests on the last three or four days preceding vacation. So again, sleep was hard to come by.

Grandma Hendley had sent the funds for Margarete's long bus ride home. As soon as the last class was over, Margarete made her way to the bus depot loaded down with packages and a few presents she had purchased. She quickly bought her ticket and boarded the bus. She was thankful that her first choice in seats was available—the very last seat next to the back door—where she could stretch out and sleep without interruption all the way to her destination of Mankato, Minnesota.

It felt like such a luxury for Margarete to be able to stretch out with no one to bother her with questions or break into her sleep. The only sounds that filled the bus were those of the other passengers quietly murmuring to each other and the steady humming of the tires on the highway. Such were the comforting, soothing sounds that lulled a tired college sophomore to sleep.

As she slept, the motion of the bus and her tossing pushed her shoulders against the back door. Suddenly, without warning, the back emergency exit door swung open with Margarete wedged against it! Her head and shoulders hung out the open door, awakening her instantly, of course, and she felt herself falling into the blackness of the night towards the hard concrete of the highway. Her first thought was, *I'm going to die!* She frantically grabbed for the door frame to catch herself but missed!

She prayed the most fervent prayer of her short life in just three words: "Jesus, help me!"

And to this day, she says she can almost still feel it—a pair of huge hands caught her and pushed her back into the bus! She quickly looked around, but no one was sitting near enough to have touched her!

When the warning light of the open door flashed red, the driver brought the bus to a quick stop and came running down the aisle to check on the problem. Stopping short, he quickly took in the sight of Margarete sitting next to the open door and leaned down to ask her, "Are you all right? I can't understand how it happened. Did you lose anything?

Are you afraid? Did you get hurt?" As you can imagine, he was more than a bit upset with the problem.

Still in a sort of shock, Margarete answered, "No sir, no problems."

"Well, then, how did you manage to hold on and not fall out?"

She replied, "I believe I had some heavenly help."

When you pass through the waters, I will be with you; and when you pass through the rivers, they will not sweep over you. When you walk through the fire, you will not be burned; the flames will not set you ablaze. For I am the Lord, your God, the Holy One of Israel, your Saviour; I give Egypt for your ransom, Cush and Seba in your stead (Isaiah 43:2-3).

FOOD FOR THOUGHT: Angels are real but not made of material substances as we are. Apparently, they have no physical nature, not even breath or blood. If they do occupy some form of permanent body, it has to be a spiritual body—apparently just like the spiritual body we shall occupy some day in eternity!

CHAPTER 37

THE DOCTOR EXPLAINS

*I*n 1965 when Joel and Jane French's son Keith was two years old, he met with what could have been a very serious accident. They were packing the car for a trip, and Keith followed them in and out of the house.

Apparently, while neither of them was watching, Keith had climbed up into the car far enough to reach the gear shift and pulled the lever out of the "park" position before he slid back down to the ground. The driveway was on a slant, and the car began to roll slowly toward the street.

Let's read their story.

From inside the house we heard Keith's screams and came running. He was lying in the driveway, and we could see black marks from the tire tread over his left leg.

We grabbed him up and rushed him to the hospital emergency room, thanking God for sparing his life as we went. Before we reached the hospital, Keith had quit crying, and he could move his leg with no apparent pain.

After examining the x-rays, the emergency room physician just shook his head in disbelief.

Then turning to us, the doctor said, "As long as I have been practicing medicine, I have never seen anything like this. The tire marks are clearly on his leg, yet he has no broken bones, no breaks in his flesh, not even a bruise. Little boy, your guardian angel was watching over you."

When the doctor explained what had happened, it was worth every cent he charged us for it. You see, at this time, we really didn't understand at all the ministry of angels as we do now. We knew God had somehow delivered Keith, but we didn't understand what part the angels played in His protection and deliverance.

The good doctor gave us the lesson in angelic help and only charged fifteen dollars for it. Well, fifteen dollars plus x-rays.

For he will command his angels concerning you to guard you in all your ways; they will lift you up in their hands, so that you will not strike your foot against a stone..."
(Psalm 91:11-12).

FOOD FOR THOUGHT: None of the stories in this book are fictional and no fictional names have been used unless there was a request for anonymity. One of the most often recurring themes when I have interviewed people is the one of angelic protection or deliverance. Right here is one of the many reasons why people find comfort in picturing a "guardian" angel who is always on duty to walk with them, shield them, protect them, keep them out of harm's way and guide them in the right direction.

SECTION 4

TRAVEL MERCIES

See, I am sending an angel ahead of you to guard you along the way and to bring you to the place I have prepared (Exodus 23:20).

CHAPTER 38

TWO WOMEN AND AN OVERHEATED CAR

essie Fisher and Nell Cheek were traveling from Memphis, Tennessee, to California by car, and they were pulling a small travel trailer. Just outside Canon City, Colorado, they decided to take the scenic Skyline Drive, which at that time was a crude gravel road, to watch the sunset.

About halfway up the first set of switchbacks, the car began losing power and slowed until it came to a stop and died. They had managed to get it to the side of the road, and Bessie jumped out and placed rocks behind the wheels of the car and trailer to keep them from rolling backwards. They raised the hood, and when Bessie naively screwed the cap off the radiator, steam and water shot out. Thankfully she didn't get scalded.

After the car cooled, they added water to the radiator from a thermos bottle and two water bags, but it still wouldn't start. Their continual cranking of the engine soon caused the battery to die too. As if their car problem wasn't enough, gnats surrounded them so they began swatting the bugs while they prayed.

During this time, two different cars passed them going down the mountain, but neither driver stopped. They simply yelled at the ladies for blocking the road. What were they to do? Nell prayed, and Bessie walked around the car, attempting to figure out the answer to their predicament. To complicate matters, the sun was now setting, and night would be quickly upon them. Their praying became more desperate, and fear began to permeate their minds.

Bessie said, "If only we could start the car, we could unhitch the trailer, turn the car around, and go back down the mountain." But the car refused to cooperate. While they were talking, a truck pulled up behind the trailer. No markings were visible on it, but they assumed it might have been a telephone truck.

The driver, wearing a white shirt and dark blue pants, stepped out of the truck and walked over to their car. Bessie began to tell him what had happened. He didn't say a word but quickly unhitched the trailer and climbed into the car. Bessie began telling him that the car wouldn't start because the battery was dead. He paid her no attention but turned the key. To the ladies' amazement, the car immediately started.

The two women watched as the man drove the car to where he could turn it around and then drove back to the trailer. He lifted the arm of the trailer, pointed it in the opposite direction, and hitched it up to the car, following the plan that the women had originally imagined might work.

As soon as his work was done, he got into his truck without even a glance over at the ladies. When Bessie walked around the trailer to ask him how much money they owed him, she was astonished to see that both the man and his truck had disappeared. The ladies were stunned. They could see well up the mountain as well as down the switchback road. There was no truck, no noise, no nothing. He had simply vanished! Who was he? How did he know they had wanted to turn the car around? How could he start the car when it had a dead battery?

The angel of the Lord encamps around those who fear him, and he delivers them (Psalm 34:7).

FOOD FOR THOUGHT: What would you do in such a set of circumstances? Pray or worry? Most of us might do both, but I would hope that we would first pray as these ladies did and watch God deliver us from our troubles.

CHAPTER 39

THE SNOWPLOW ANGEL

*D*uring the winter of 1987, John and Roberta (names changed) were in a crisis! Their four-year-old son, Benjamin, became deathly sick. What had started out as a cold had turned into the flu and eventually became a severe case of full-blown pneumonia. His fever elevated to 104°, and he became delirious, drifting in and out of consciousness. The nearest hospital was more than thirty miles from the family's Colorado ranch near Glenwood Springs. That's not too far when road conditions are good, but when your child needs immediate help and a western snowstorm is raging outside, it's like a thousand miles away. The doctor advised them to get Benjamin to the hospital as quickly as possible, if it was possible at all since all roads in and out of Glenwood Springs were blocked by snowdrifts.

John prepared his truck, a four-wheel-drive Ford F-350 with chains, extra blankets, lots of hot coffee, road flares, a shovel, some food, and emergency candles. Even with these provisions, however, it would be a tough trip. He backed out of the shed and slid to a stop by the side door where Roberta was anxiously waiting with Benjamin all bundled up to protect him from the bitter cold. Before they started on their perilous journey to the hospital, John prayed a simple, desperate prayer for help: "Lord, you see our need. Benjamin is sick and could die. Watch over us and protect us on our mission of mercy. Amen."

Along the way, they encountered drifts as high as six or seven feet and had to break right through them on the two miles of gravel road that led to the highway. Their hopes soared when they discovered the main road had recently been plowed and they would be able to cover the next fifteen miles with no trouble. But then the road conditions abruptly changed for the worse. As they looked to the right, their hearts fell as they saw the snowplow, broken down and buried in drifting snow. The road ahead was covered everywhere with at least three feet of snow with drifts of six or seven feet. They had little choice, so they continued on, although their progress was slow.

Suddenly Eric shouted, "Oh, no!" The truck tilted hard to the right and dropped into a hole. A part of the highway had collapsed, leaving a four foot gaping hole into which the truck's front end had dropped with the frame resting on the edge of the pavement. Their journey seemed finished. They were stuck and Glenwood Springs was still seven miles away! Eric prayed again, "Lord, I've not asked for much. Can You help us now? Amen!"

Soon, they heard the sounds of a heavy diesel engine behind them—it was the broken down snowplow at work once again! John told Roberta everything would be okay and ran back to meet the plow. A young man was driving and had a huge smile for John as he asked, "Can you help us?"

The man replied, "That's why I'm here." A chain was quickly attached to the Ford pickup, and the truck was pulled out. There was no serious damage to the undercarriage, so the young man said, "Follow me. I'll plow the road for you." In what seemed like no time at all, they reached the city limits and pulled into the hospital parking lot. When they got Benjamin safely inside, the doctors said they had arrived just in time. Had they been delayed any longer, he might not have survived. Benjamin recovered, and John gave the credit to the snowplow driver.

To show his appreciation, John called the county maintenance office and asked for the supervisor. When he came on the line, John told him what had happened and asked for the driver's name because they owed him so much and wanted to personally express their appreciation.

There was a long pause on the line and the supervisor finally said, "Well, sir, the snowplow you're talking about is driven by Lonnie Mickes, but he's not here. His truck busted a transmission yesterday about seven miles out of town. It's still sitting out there, so Lonnie went home. He won't be back in until tomorrow morning when we hope to have another rig ready for him to use."

Praise the Lord, you his angels, you mighty ones who do his bidding, who obey his word. Praise the Lord, all his heavenly hosts, you his servants who do his will. Praise the Lord, all his works everywhere in his dominion. Praise the Lord, O my soul (Psalm 103:20-22).

FOOD FOR THOUGHT: Angels can get so absorbed in their work that their appearance is dictated by their special assignment. Depending upon their assigned task in serving us, they may remain invisible or appear in ordinary human form. Their form depends on their function in the mission they have been sent on to accomplish. J. M. Wilson wrote, "In general they are simply regarded as embodiments of their mission."

CHAPTER 40

CHANGING TIRES

*P*astor George L. Greer was driving alone from Mabank, Texas, to Dallas for a special ministers' meeting. While on the rather long and lonely stretch of highway between Mabank and Kaufman, he suddenly realized he had a flat tire. He immediately pulled the car off the pavement, glided to a stop, and got out to inspect the damage. The rear tire was completely flat and would have to be changed. He opened the trunk only to discover that he had no jack. What was he to do?

The area was new to him, and he didn't know how far he would have to walk for help. (This was a few decades before cell phones appeared on the scene.) He looked up and down the highway, but no cars, gas stations, or even a farmhouse could be seen. Only wide open fields and grazing land surrounded him.

Suddenly from what seemed to be out of nowhere, a Jeep type of vehicle pulled up, and two young men leaped out and stood by his side.

Speaking quite rapidly but kindly, one of them said, "We see you have a problem, Reverend, and we have come to help you." They immediately produced a jack and tire tools, and went to work. When the pastor offered to help, the spokesman said, "No, no, sir; you will only get your clothes dirty, and it is our business to help pastors."

While they were quickly changing the tire, a rather strange feeling began to come over George. He went to the front of the car to check both tires. While he was kneeling down, the two young men had finished changing the rear flat. He stood up and turned to thank them, but no one was there! Both the young men and their vehicle had simply vanished. He looked up and down the highway, but no one was in sight. The road was flat for miles in each direction, and no one could be seen.

Could they have been angels, he thought. Then a sense of a special presence stayed with him during this entire day and remained with him late into the evening when he was able to relate the experience to his wife, Lucy.[1]

Are not all angels ministering spirits sent to serve those who will inherit salvation? (Hebrews 1:14)

FOOD FOR THOUGHT: I am always amazed at such stories. Where did the angels come from? How did they know they were changing the tire of a clergyman? How can a car materialize and then simply disappear? Do angels have some kind of mechanical training? Are there cars in heaven? My humanness and curiosity have more questions than answers. How about you? The only conclusion is that we are to live by faith and believe by faith in the Word of God as to the reality of angels and how they have been created to be ministering spirits for our benefit.

1 Adapted from Lucy I. Greer, *Reflections of Faith, Vol. II*, Assemblies of God Benevolence Dept., Springfield, MO. Used by permission.

CHAPTER 41

THE MIRACLE IN SKAGWAY

*P*auline Pratt and her husband were ministers of music in Calvary Temple in Denver. During this time they spent a two-week vacation on the Alaskan Highway and had quite an unusual experience. Let's let Pauline tell us their story.

We were traveling with missionary friends who were on their way to Point Barrow, Alaska. The beauty of this scene was awesome. We camped in our tent each night, listening to the sound of wild animals all around us; and in the morning, we could see their footprints. There was almost no darkness during the evenings because of the midnight sun. An added bonus was the availability of wild berries that we picked by the bucketful.

After we parted from our friends, we boarded a scenic train to Skagway. We arrived there only to discover that the airlines were on strike, and all the chartered boats from Skagway were booked solid. We were stranded there with no way out.

What were we to do? We started walking around this small town, and a few blocks from the railway station we came upon a small building with a sign that indicated it was a mission. Intrigued we went to the side door and knocked.

A woman opened the door and to our amazement said, "Come on in, Brother and Sister Pratt." We were stunned for we had never met her before. She continued, "An angel of the Lord told me you were coming, gave me your names, and said that I should immediately prepare dinner for you. I have it all ready!"

We could already smell the wonderful aroma of the dinner and see that the table was set and ready for us. We were dumbfounded!

Adding to our further amazement, she continued, "I know you don't have much faith, but when you go to the tourist travel office in the morning, you will find that they have tickets for you and your wife."

My husband quietly said, "But we have just come from there, and they were fully booked."

We had a delightful dinner and learned that our hosts were missionaries to the Eskimo people of the area. In the morning we were awakened to the smell of coffee brewing and bacon frying. It was a great time of food, fun, and good fellowship. After breakfast our hostess abruptly turned to my husband and said, "Now you need to go immediately and pick up your tickets at the travel office. The fare is considerably more than the cash you have with you, so take this $200 and pay me back after you get home."

We said goodbye to our new friends and went on our way, marveling at the events that had just occurred. As we entered the travel office, the man at the desk said, "We've been trying to find you...the strangest thing just happened. A couple took the train over to White Horse yesterday and called just now to say they planned on staying longer than they anticipated. And so they canceled their tickets on the boat "Princess Kathleen." He smiled and added, "That has never happened to us!"

> *Praise the Lord you his angels, you mighty ones who do his bidding, who obey his word* (Psalm 103:20).

FOOD FOR THOUGHT: I am always amazed at such happenings. My analytical mind attempts to figure out a logical reason for how this might have happened. Doesn't God have more important matters to take care of in His universe than helping two people in need? I always come back to the answer that it's our God at work once more, helping out people who are stranded and need assistance. Faith is the only thing that supplies an answer.

CHAPTER 42

ANGEL ON A TRACTOR

*I*n September of 2002, DuWayne Paul took a leap of faith that opened the door for an unusual encounter with an angel half a world away.

While he was attending a men's retreat at Camp Shamineau, near Motley, Minnesota, a presentation was given about the English language camps that were held for the past ten years in Poland and Austria. (The camps have helped spur a revival among many young people in these countries.)

An announcement was made at the retreat that the Chinese government had invited Shamineau International to hold their first camp in rural China in the summer of 2003. DuWayne felt that the Holy Spirit was urging him to volunteer to go, and so he did.

In August of 2003, a group of twenty men and women set off from the U.S.A. bound for Hailar, China, near the Russian and Mongolian borders in northeast China. It was quite a journey, taking them two days to get there by planes, trains, and finally in buses (really twenty-passenger vans).

When they arrived, they piled into three vans along with some forty Chinese people, children, guides and drivers.

DuWayne tells the story:

On the way to the camp, in a very rural part of China about twenty miles south of Hailar, we encountered a road leading to the camp that was under construction for improvements. For several weeks, all traffic on this road had been detoured through a nearby field. However, it had been raining for two solid weeks, and the field was now nothing but mud and sticky Chinese clay. Attempting to follow the tracks of previous traffic through the field, eventually all three vans became so stuck in the mud that it was impossible to go any further. We did all we could to get ourselves unstuck; the men pushing the van couldn't even begin to budge the wheels. We couldn't go forward nor could we back up; we were stuck dead in our tracks. There were no signs of life three or four miles in any direction and no farms or houses anywhere. We were completely isolated.

The American leaders gathered in the front bus to pray and ask God how to proceed. We considered walking back to the nearest village for help and then attempt to find another place where we could hold the camp.

While we were still praying, a gentleman in our group looked up and said, "We can stop praying; our answer is here!"

We opened our eyes and saw a brand new 7000 series four-wheel drive John Deere tractor approaching! We could hardly believe the swift answer to prayer we had just received. The driver stopped and cheerfully offered to help us. He proceeded to pull our vans out of the mud, one by one, and onto some nearby grass where we were able to get traction. He assisted us with a smile on his face, and when he was finished, he abruptly left in the same direction from which he had come. We were so grateful for his help with the tractor that we formed a circle and expressed our thanks to God before we hurriedly piled back into the vans.

We watched the man on the tractor slowly drive over the crest of a small hill until he was out of our line of sight. We started our vans and followed the man over the same hill. When we came to the top, we expected to see the tractor just ahead, but the entire landscape was empty—the tractor had vanished! From the top of the hill, we could see four or five miles in every direction, but the tractor had disappeared without a trace.

When we discussed the startling events of the day, we decided that we had at least four good reasons to believe that our help was heaven sent, and the man was an angel on a John Deere! First of all, this was grasslands country, and we saw no trace of farming or agriculture in the area. Someone took a picture of the tractor, and empty landscape surrounds us. The tractor had no reason whatsoever to be at this particular place. Second, all the tractors we had seen earlier and would see in the coming days were like small garden tractors. We never saw anything approaching the 7000 series John Deere either in newness or size.

From the picture it is also obvious that there is no mud on the tires of the tractor! This was just not possible because of the muddy conditions of the road and the field where we were stuck. Fourth, the kindly Chinese gentleman on the tractor refused to take any money for his efforts—definitely very un-Chinese-like.

We came to the conclusion that we had experienced an angelic intervention. But this was not the end of the story. We enjoyed our two weeks of conducting the English language study camp in which we taught Chinese children English, based on our American holidays such as Christmas, Easter, Memorial, and the Fourth of July. We were able to share many eternal truths during the camp.

After returning home, I received an e-mail from one of the Chinese missionaries who served as our guide. I had sent him a CD with all my digital pictures from the trip. He sent me the following astonishing message:

> Would you believe it? Upon magnifying the photo of the tractor that pulled your buses out of the mud in Hulun-Beier, I found that the brand name on the hood of the tractor is *Di-Er Tian-Tuo*. *Di-Er* is a transliteration for Deere and *Tian-Tuo* is a shortened version of *Tian-Tuo-La-ji*, which literally means, "Tractor From Heaven"!

There you have it: "(John) Deere Tractor From Heaven." Incredible! God was with us that day and certainly did not want us to turn back. The events of the two weeks at the camp and the impact on so many young lives would never have happened if we had turned back because of the mud. I believe to this day that we actually met an angel driving a John Deere tractor in rural northeast China!

They passed the first and second guards and came to the iron gate leading to the city. It opened for them by itself, and they went through it. When they had walked the length of one street, suddenly the angel left him (Acts 12:10).

FOOD FOR THOUGHT: What an incredible angelic encounter! How often is an intervention documented by photos and about sixty witnesses who experienced it together? You may have lots of questions about where the tractor came from and so forth, but there can be no questions about the reality of this encounter. God is still alive today, and His angelic hosts are also alive and well. Take this at face value and praise the Lord for His goodness.

Actual photo of the "Deere Tractor From Heaven" and our heavenly helper

CHAPTER 43

SURVIVING A PLANE CRASH

*N*orman Williams tells the story of being one of the few survivors of one of the world's worst aircraft disasters. There were 653 passengers on two jumbo jets that collided on Canary Island, March 27, 1977—593 were killed and only 60 survived. How he escaped from this fiery crash is nothing short of a miracle. Norm begins:

The day we left Los Angeles, my widowed mother, who has lived with me for eighteen years, prayed for traveling mercies for me. As she prayed she began to weep, and this startled me because this was the first time I'd ever seen her crying like that. She was weeping so bitterly that she couldn't conclude the prayer.

At the airport, while we were waiting on the plane for our turn to take off, a KLM plane taxied by my window only to disappear into the fog. A few minutes later, our 747 slowly taxied down the same runway. The KLM jet was to taxi to the end of the runway and then turn around and take off down the same runway. We were supposed to go partway

134

down this runway and veer off onto a side ramp to wait for our turn to take off.

Before we arrived at the side ramp, our pilot saw the lights of the KLM in the distance. Of course, he thought these lights were stationary. As he continued to taxi out on the runway, suddenly to his complete horror, he realized those lights were not stationary but were coming toward us at the full takeoff speed of approximately 200 miles per hour. He tried desperately to get our 747 off the runway, but he didn't make it.

When the jet came roaring out of the fog and saw our plane, the KLM pilot decided the only possible evasive action was to attempt to take off over our plane. He got the nose of his plane over us, but the landing gear didn't make it and came slicing through our jet like a hot butcher knife going through butter. Our plane was cut in half just a few rows in front of me in the tourist section. The front part of the plane fell forward, and most of the people that survived were in that section. In our center section very few people lived, and in the tail section no one survived.

Immediately on impact, thousands of gallons of jet fuel came gushing through our section like a gigantic wave. Many people were saturated with the fuel and became flaming torches just seconds later. I unfastened my seatbelt and stood up as explosions and fire engulfed the plane. To my left in the window seat was an eighty-six-year-old woman and next to her in the center seat was her sixty-five-year-old daughter. Immediately in front of me, in the aisle seat, was my business partner, Ted. As I stood in the aisle, I looked to see if I could help the mother and daughter. It was too late. They were on fire and obviously dead. I couldn't see Ted.

People were burning to death all around me. I could smell their hair burning and hear their screams. The cabin was a furnace, and the thick smoke made seeing and breathing difficult. Flying debris had slashed into the flesh of the passengers, and the sound of crushing, grinding, exploding metal was terrifying. It was hell on earth, and it all happened in a matter of seconds!

In the midst of this inferno, I could hear agonizing calls for help, mingled with loud cursing as people burned to death. It shocked me to hear cursing because I thought if people were facing death, they would automatically call on God. (From this experience, I now believe people die as they live.)

I have been a Christian since 1932, and now as the roaring flames seared those around me, portions of Scripture flashed through my mind, "I will never leave you or forsake you...I am the God that will deliver you... Fear not for I have redeemed you...When you walk through the fire I will be with you!"

I began calling aloud to God: "I stand on Your Word...I stand on Your Word!" As I repeated those five words, I saw a large chunk of debris hurtling toward me, and I put up both arms and shoved it away with supernatural strength. When I did this, I looked up for the first time since the crash and saw a large hole in the ceiling of the plane. The ceilings in 747s are more than ten feet high, but somehow I climbed up through that hole. The metal was razor sharp and jagged, shredding my hands. It later took forty stitches to save my fingers that were nearly slashed off.

It was a miracle that I was able to hurl my body through the hole and over those sharp edges. When you're fifty-two and weigh 260 pounds, you just don't do things like that anymore. Once I cleared the hole, I fell and landed on the wing. Keeping my balance was difficult because the wing was tilted and extremely slippery with jet fuel. The engines were still running, and fire was raging in them. I knew the wing was full of fuel and that it would be only a matter of seconds before the whole thing would go because I could hear small explosions inside. I worked my way out on the wing and jumped to the ground. I'm told I fell about thirty feet. When I landed, I shattered the bones in my left foot but was able to hobble away from the plane. I heard two large explosions, and when I looked back, our entire plane was gone!

I looked down the runway 150 yards and saw the KLM exploding violently. There were 250 passengers on that plane. No one left in the plane got out of it alive![1]

But now, this is what the Lord says... "Fear not, for I have redeemed you; I have summoned you by name; you are mine. When you pass through the waters, I will be with you; and when you pass through the rivers, they will not sweep over you. When you walk through the fire, you will not be burned; the flames will not set you ablaze. For I am the Lord, your God, the Holy One of Israel, your Savior" (Isaiah 43:1-3).

FOOD FOR THOUGHT: What mysterious force could have picked up the 260 pound, fifty-two-year-old Norman Williams and propelled him more than ten feet straight up through the top of the fuselage of that burning 747? I vote for a "travel mercies" angel who was on duty in that moment! How about you?

1 Norman Williams, "Terror at Tenerife," *VOICE*, April 1979, Full Gospel Business Men's Fellowship International, Costa Mesa, California, condensed.

CHAPTER 44

DO WE ALL HAVE
A GUARDIAN ANGEL?

*W*e'll answer that question after we first read what Lester Sumrall wrote:

Some years ago I was traveling with a group up near the border of Tibet. Somehow, I became lost...I mean absolutely lost! You know the feeling. I was separated from my party from early morning until about 4:30 that afternoon. I was in a little Chinese village all by myself, without knowing one word of their language. I was sad, lost, and tired.

Then I noticed a young man come riding through the gates on a majestic horse, quite different from the mountain mules we were using. He rode right up to me, dismounted, and began to speak in perfect English.

"Where did you come from?" I asked. "How is it that you speak English so beautifully?"

He smiled and replied, "I know the party you're looking for. I met them on the road. If you go out this gate and then travel for about two hours on this path, you'll find them."

I took his advice. I got on my mule, headed out the gate, and sure enough, before too long I found the folks with whom I had been traveling. I inquired of them about the young man. They hadn't seen him and didn't know anything about him! I'm positive it was my guardian angel!

I cannot prove conclusively from the Bible the existence of your own personal guardian angel. However, some references, when taken together, seem to strongly suggest this possibility. At least, I am convinced.

Let's start with Psalm 91:11,

> *For He will command His angels concerning YOU to guard YOU in all YOUR ways; they will lift YOU up in their hands...*(emphasis mine).

Notice that these pronouns are all singular! This goes along with the concept we have of a God who is always very much aware of our needs and concerns and is able to minister to us in our needs.

Come with me to the Old Testament where a dying Jacob was blessing his grandchildren, Joseph's sons. The setting is found in Genesis 48:15-16.

> *Then he blessed Joseph and said, "May the God before whom my fathers Abraham and Isaac walked, the God who has been MY shepherd all MY life to this day, the ANGEL who has delivered ME from all harm—may he bless these boys"* (emphasis mine).

Was that a guardian angel who had watched over Jacob in his many adventures of his life? I like to think it was.

How close is your personal angel when you might need him? There is an answer in Psalm 34:7.

The angel of the Lord encamps around those who fear him, and he delivers them!

This verse literally means your angel puts up his tent around you, if you fear the Lord. You don't have to worry about leaving him behind on your next plane trip!

Let's not overlook little children or think they are not very important in God's plans. It was Jesus Himself who in Matthew 18:10 said,

See that you do not look down on one of these little ones. For I tell you that THEIR ANGELS in heaven always see the face of my Father in heaven (emphasis mine).

That's the strongest biblical suggestion that each child and by inference, each person, has a guardian angel all his or her own. Maybe it's because little kids need more angelic protection than adults.

As I looked, thrones were set in place, and the Ancient of Days took his seat. His clothing was as white as snow; the hair of his head was white like wool. His throne was flaming with fire, and its wheels were all ablaze. A river of fire was flowing, coming out from before him. THOUSANDS UPON THOUSANDS attended Him; TEN THOUSAND TIMES TEN THOUSAND stood before him (Daniel 7:9-10 emphasis mine).

FOOD FOR THOUGHT: Perhaps you are thinking: *There are more than six billion people on this earth and that number is growing. Are there enough angels to go around?* If you believe that God has assigned a private, guardian angel to you and me, then surely, there must be more than enough angels to go around and do the job. They were created by God in the beginning and if He runs short, surely He can create more!

CHAPTER 45

ALMOST OVER THE CLIFF

Mayme E. Williams of Durant, Florida, and a coworker had a harrowing experience while they were driving through the mountains in upper New York. Mayme shares the following story:

The trip to the summit was without incident, but as we started down the other side it happened. We hit a patch of loose gravel that had somehow been dumped on top of the paved road, and our car began to skid in the direction of the precipice!

At this instant, we both saw an angel standing on the edge of the cliff directly in front of our skidding car. The angel was tall, dressed in white, and raised his hand with a commanding gesture for the car to stop. We knocked over the guard rail and came to a stop with one wheel hanging slightly over the very edge of the cliff. The car stopped with such a jolt that the box of cherries on the seat between us was so scattered that for weeks afterward I found some of them below the dash and under the front seat when we removed it.

Of course, we were very shaken but managed to carefully get out of the car and survey our plight. My coworker stood so gripped with fear she couldn't move and refused to get back into the car. She was convinced the extra weight would take the car over the cliff. God gave me the courage to get in the car and back it away from the cliff. What really helped me was the angel's presence—I saw him standing in front of the car while I started it. He appeared to be holding up the right front fender and wheel.

Fortunately neither of us was hurt in any way—no bumps, no bruises, nothing—but as a reminder of our episode, the bumper needed to be repaired as well as the right front fender. The damage was so slight that we were able to continue on to our destination without any other incidents.

That was a mountain angel, I presume. This same gracious lady has another angel story to share with us:

I must tell you of one more narrow escape. This happened in the Philippines while the Communists were attempting a coup. They had blockaded this particular town at both ends of the highway, and no one could get through. They laid in wait to ambush people as they traveled from Manila to the north and killed all whom they ambushed.

An angel of the Lord appeared and told me to leave this town and return to Manila and the promised protection there. That day as I left town for Manila, I reached the dangerous area, which was in control of the Communists. The Lord sent such a storm of rain I could hardly keep the car on the road as we traveled for miles through the guerilla controlled area. But when we got safely through there, our special escort and cover—the rain—stopped as suddenly as it had started, and we arrived home safely!

In my life, time and time again, God has given us proof of the faithfulness of His promises of protection and care!

The angel of the Lord encamps around those who fear him, and he delivers them. Taste and see that the Lord is good; blessed is the man who takes refuge in him (Psalm 34:7-8).

FOOD FOR THOUGHT: What do angels do? We know they worship God and bring judgments, but they can also give us information, bring encouragement, do battle for God, and protect believers. This protection of believers may be the most common of angelic actions. What an experience to have witnessed such acts of protection as our two stories above have illustrated!

CHAPTER 46

FOOTPRINTS IN THE SNOW

*D*oreene Upton of Wildwood, Florida, will never forget her experience with an angel. Along with her sister, Evelyn age twenty-two, and Mildred Morneau, a very good friend, age nineteen, Doreene, herself just eighteen, had just finished providing the singing and preaching at a small church in Rothsay, Minnesota in the middle of winter. Let's have her tell her story:

During the church service, an old fashioned, white-out, blowing, drifting, Minnesota blizzard had swooped down on us. When it was time to leave, we looked out into the night. Yes, it was bad—visibility was almost down to zero. But we needed to return home to Pelican Rapids about twenty-six miles away so we could get ready for another engagement in Jenkins the next day.

The pastor pleaded with us not to leave in the storm, but we persisted. My sister insisted that we could make it back home no matter how bad the weather because we were "Minnesota natives" and knew how to drive in such stuff. The wind was blowing, and more than a foot of snow blanketed the ground with much more piling up in drifts.

Evelyn started our 1926 Dodge, and we headed for home. We drove through the snow and hit drifts as deep as the radiator cap. Soon we were bucking drifts which needed more than one attempt for us to plow through them. We stopped, backed up, and hit them again. Even though we went slowly, it was still really difficult to see where the road was.

Soon we hit a drift we couldn't barrel through and we couldn't even back away from it. We were stuck! We came to the conclusion that we had left the road and wandered into a field. We decided there was nothing to do but have a real prayer meeting. We felt we could pray better on our knees so Mildred climbed into the backseat and fell on her knees, Evelyn and I knelt on the floorboards in the front seat, and we began to pray! I mean we really prayed! We were well aware of our dangerous situation—we could freeze; we were lost; no one would know we were missing so no one would be out to rescue us. Yes, we had a real prayer meeting!

When we finished, Evelyn started the old Dodge and backed up for another run through the drift; this time, we broke through easily. But the problem remained, where was the road? Then, all three of us saw large red footprints! At first we thought they might have been left by some kind of wounded animal bleeding on the snow. But Mildred said, "No, they're large footprints!" They were bright red and we could just make them out a few feet in front of our car, illuminated by our headlights. Mildred said, "I know we are to follow them!"

And so, slowly, Evelyn drove the car, following the path that the footprints had made. We hit many more drifts, but not one of them stopped us. We drove as easily as though there were no snowdrifts on the road. It was a miracle of deliverance! It was as if the road had been plowed clean even though we went through drifts that came up over the hood of the car.

What is so amazing is the footprints led us all the way home, approximately twenty miles. They led us up our driveway and all the way to our parking spot next to the humble house we were renting! When we got out of the car we looked behind us and saw our tire tracks, but no more red footprints! Who made such huge footprints? We came to the conclusion that it was something from the spiritual world and concluded it had been an angel with huge red feet sent on a mission of mercy and help!

For he will command his angels concerning you to guard you in all your ways; they will lift you up in their hands, so that you will not strike your foot against a stone (Psalm 91:11-12).

FOOD FOR THOUGHT: It seems to me, angels must always be on duty in good days as well as bad days when the storms of life hit. Of course they are not subject to the same laws of nature that we are, so an angel who leaves tracks in the snow will not freeze to death. They are more than able to rescue us in our need, no matter what kind of day it is.

CHAPTER 47

JUST IN TIME

The crack British express train raced through the night, its powerful headlight spearing through the fog and the darkness ahead. This was a special run because it was carrying Queen Victoria and her entourage.

Suddenly, the engineer saw a startling sight. Revealed in the beam of the engine's headlight was a strange figure loosely wrapped in a black coat flapping in the breeze. It was standing in the middle of the train tracks, waving its arms and signaling the train to stop. The engineer immediately grabbed the brakes and brought the train to a screeching, grinding, sparks-flying halt.

The engineer, his assistant, the coal tender, and a couple of conductors climbed down to see what had stopped them. They looked all around but could find no trace of the strange figure. On a hunch, the engineer walked some yards further down the tracks. Instantly he stopped and stared into the fog in horror. The rainstorm, which had passed through the area earlier in the evening, had caused the bridge to wash out in the middle section and topple into the storm-swollen stream.

If he had not paid attention to the ghostly, weird figure, the train would have plunged into the overflowing stream, and many lives would have been lost and bodies mangled. Who knows, perhaps even the Queen herself would have been killed or injured. The engineer was so overcome with emotion of the near miss, he sat down on the tracks for some time before making his way back to the idling steam engine.

Word was wired ahead for help. While they were waiting for it to arrive, the crew unsuccessfully made a more intensive search for the strange flagman.

Eventually they got the train and passengers back to the station in London and solved the mystery of the strange figure. At the base of the steam engine's headlight, the engineer discovered a huge dead moth. He looked at it a few moments, and on impulse, wet its wings and pasted it to the glass of the headlamp. Climbing back into the cab, he switched on the lamp and saw the "flagman" in the beam. He had the answer now to the strange flagman—the moth had flown into the beam mere seconds before the train was due to reach the washed-out bridge. In the fog it had appeared to be a phantom figure, a flagman waving its arms signaling the train to stop!

Later, when Queen Victoria was told of the strange happenings and the discovery of what the strange, weird flagman had apparently been, she thought a moment or two. She said, "I'm sure it was no accident. It was God's way of protecting us. He sent an angel in the form of a moth to warn us."

Angels come in various sizes, shapes, and forms, in whatever way we need them to come. The main thing is that God sends them for our care and protection.

Praise the Lord, you his angels, you mighty ones who do his bidding, who obey his word" (Psalm 103:20).

FOOD FOR THOUGHT: If you happen to be a skeptic at heart you can shoot this story full of holes. You might say that it was nothing but a coincidence or just a chance happening. Or you can simply believe that the "coincidence" might be God at work, wishing to remain anonymous. I choose the later. What other explanation could you put forward that makes as much sense?

CHAPTER 48

THE WARNING

*O*n this typical school day morning, Ruthie Osterhus (names changed) was making the regular drive with her two kids to Eugene Field Elementary School. The kids were doing their usual bickering and fighting on the short ride. This morning would be different.

Ruthie was attempting to cope with a migraine headache, and her patience was in short supply.

Shouts kept coming from the backseat, "Mommie, he's grabbing my lunch box!" was the scream of eight-year-old Lisa.

"Did not!" shouted her nine-year-old son Tommy with just as much volume.

"Enough! Stop it!" Ruthie shouted into the back seat, "No more of it, both of you!"

It was like shouting to the wind.

"There, he did it again!" cried Lisa.

Now, Ruthie gripped the wheel tighter, knuckles turning whiter, anger rising, but then she breathed a prayer, "Please, Lord, help me make it this last half mile."

Quietly at first, then building with each repeat came the taunt, "Lisa is a tattletale! Lisa is a tattletale! Lisa is a tattletale!"

"He's teasing me! Make him stop, Mommie!" came the reply from Lisa.

At that, Ruthie partially turned her head and scolded both of them vehemently.

Then Ruthie distinctly heard a loud voice she had never heard before. It commanded: "RUTHIE! STOP! QUICK! NOW!"

Stunned at the forcefulness of this strange voice, Ruthie quickly turned back to the road, and there was a stop sign dead ahead! It was a four-way intersection. She slammed on her brakes, and the car skidded, squealing to a violent stop. The seatbelts were the only restraint keeping the kids from being pitched into the front seat or windshield.

In a fraction of a second after the stop, an old battered pick-up, loaded with junk, plowed through the stop sign on her left at a high rate of speed. The driver then lost control and veered hard right, hit the curb and the truck overturned, spilling its contents all over the street!

Other motorists rushed to help the pickup driver. Ruthie, still with the steering wheel in her white-knuckle grasp just sat there; then she began to shake. One other driver approached her car, and she put down the window and asked, "Is he hurt?"

"A little more shook up than anything. He'll be all right." Then he added, "Lady, I saw it all. It's a good thing you stopped when you did. That guy would have nailed you broadside. The angels sure must have been riding with you today, lady, is all I can say."

Okay, you tell me. It wasn't an appearance of an angel, so where did the voice come from? Oh, yes, the kids said they heard the voice too. What other explanations can you offer for this intervention in the normal course of human events?

Whether you turn to the right or to the left, your ears will hear a voice behind you, saying, "This is the way; walk in it" (Isaiah 30:21).

FOOD FOR THOUGHT: Well, here we are again. How do you explain such a happening? Either you believe in a supernatural intervention or you can go on searching for a plausible explanation. Yes, I know, it does take a little bit of faith to believe angels are the answer. It takes no faith to kick it all to pieces. Let's let David Ben Gurion have the final word on this situation: "Any man who does not believe in miracles is not a realist."

CHAPTER 49

WHAT POLICEMAN?

The Curtis Steen family from Idaho was traveling on I-35 through Iowa in a typical winter snowstorm. As they traveled, the storm increased in its fury. Travel was slow and harrowing in the blowing and drifting snow. They decided to keep on going so they could reach their destination on time. They were also thinking and hoping they might be out of the storm by the time they reached the Missouri border.

But of real immediate concern to them at the moment was the gas gauge in their car. It registered empty! They had stopped in a couple of towns only to find the storm had closed down everything, including gas stations. The only solution was for the family to begin praying for help.

It became absolutely critical that they find fuel, or they would be stuck out on the road in the storm. At the next small town exit, they turned off and went again in search of help. A town police officer pulled alongside their car and motioned them to lower their window. He asked them if they needed anything.

Curtis replied, "We're just about out of gas." The officer told them to follow him to a gas station to which he had a key, and he would help them get some gas, even though it was closed.

They followed him and fueled up their car. When they went to pay him, he refused their money. Relieved to have gas once again in their car, they drove off. They had not gone far when Lou Ann spoke up from the back seat, "We didn't thank the man for his help." In their rush to get back on the road, they had neglected this courtesy, and their little daughter reminded them.

So they turned around before they reached the highway and drove right back to the station, only to find that it must have been abandoned for years. Now they were really intrigued and mystified.

They decided to track down the town police officer who had helped them. They drove around without any success until they stopped a man who was out on his snowmobile. They told him they were looking for the town cop, who had been so helpful to them, because they wanted to express their thanks before getting back on the interstate.

The snowmobile rider told them the town had never had a town cop and certainly did not have one now.

What an exciting story! The more I collect, catalog, interview, research and write angel stories the more intrigued I am about the fabulous variety and endless opportunities in these encounters. Think about this miracle. Where did the gas come from? Where did the electricity come from to pump the gas into the tank? Where did the policeman come from?

How did the car materialize, the one he was driving? How did the abandoned station come back to life for those few moments? And how did the angel learn how to drive a car? All I can say in response to these questions is to use the word lots of young ones use: awesome!

Jesus did many other miraculous signs in the presence of his disciples, which are not recorded in this book. But these are written that you may believe that Jesus is the Christ, the son of God, and that by believing you may have life in his name (John 20:30-31).

FOOD FOR THOUGHT: I think a quote from the pen of Hope MacDonald has a thought for those of us who may have never encountered angels: "We may not experience the supernatural deliverance of an angel, but God promises us supernatural strength of spirit." If angels are part of our miraculous deliverance, wonderful! But what if angels don't appear? Simply remember, God has always promised His presence with us. Angels are wonderful, but God is greater!

CHAPTER 50

NO SUCH ADDRESS

I often marvel at the great variety of angel stories people have shared with me. Some border on the edge of being totally unbelievable were it not for the supernatural element that makes them possible. Russell F. DeHart of Fruita, Colorado, shares such a story.

We were driving through Arizona on our way back home from a family vacation in California. The family had quieted down and everyone was either asleep or very nearly there. It was a calm, clear, hot night in Arizona. I preferred to cover some of this stretch of highway at night because of the intense heat during the day. The trip was going along nicely when I noticed the temperature gauge on the dashboard began to rise. Soon it was indicating an overheating engine, and we needed help quickly.

Fortunately, I managed to get the car to the next exit where there happened to be a small mini-mart and combination gas pump. I pulled in and inquired about some help. The attendant assured me no help would be available until morning anywhere in the area, and furthermore he didn't know of any mechanics in the area. We were stuck in a pretty remote location with the next service station miles away.

All of a sudden, a man stepped up from an aisle in the store. I hadn't noticed anybody else around when I entered the store and didn't know how or when he could have made his appearance. The store attendant seemed also surprised to see someone else in the store. This strange man asked me what was wrong with my car.

I replied, "My car is overheating, and I'm not quite sure what is wrong. I need to get it to a mechanic or a garage for some help."

He said, "Well, just follow me to my house. I'll give you some help. It's not far, just a couple of blocks, and I'm sure it won't hurt your car to drive such a short distance."

I really had no other choice. He seemed to be a nice man, but you know how it is when you're away from home and in a strange place with strange people. However, despite my fears I followed him.

We pulled up into his driveway, and he went for some tools. In a very quick amount of time, our car was fixed. He produced some antifreeze to replace the coolant I had lost, and we were ready to get underway again. I was surprised at how little time it had taken. I attempted to pay the man for his time and materials, but he absolutely refused to take anything.

As we drove out of his place, we took down the address and house number from his mailbox as well as his name. After we arrived home, I sent him a special "thank you" card and more than enough money to cover the costs. In a few days the note was returned and marked: "No such person known" and "No such address."

We were puzzled but thought no more about it. A few months later we had to make another quick trip to California and pass through this same town. We decided to take the note and the money, and track down this helpful stranger.

We drove into town and began looking for the house. We found the street but could not find the house nor the house number. We inquired down at the courthouse, showing them the name and the house number. The clerk replied, "No such person has ever lived in this town, and no house was ever built at the address you have given me."

Russell said in recounting the story, "I firmly believe this man was an angel sent to help us."

Are not all angels ministering spirits sent to serve those who will inherit salvation? (Hebrews 1:14)

FOOD FOR THOUGHT: I love the word picture painted here by the writer of the Book of Hebrews—angels are ministering spirits. A "ministering" being is one who attends to needs, serves, answers, obliges, tends, and takes care of someone in need. Awesome!

CHAPTER 51

THE EMERGENCY CALL

*L*ou is a very busy, workaholic type of entrepreneur who also makes time in his hectic life for community service. He enjoys being a volunteer fireman because he loves to be of help, and the challenge of fighting fires had always been something he wanted to do.

This particular week had been a very busy one. He had closed his shop early on Saturday afternoon so he and his employees could kick back and relax. He had other things on his mind—his beloved team's football game. That afternoon was going to be a time for him to lean back in his recliner chair in front of his large screen TV set and watch football for the rest of the afternoon.

Just before halftime the phone rang, and reluctantly he picked it up. It was an emergency fire call, and he was needed immediately!

He grabbed his fire fighting gear and ran out the door to his pickup parked in the driveway. He flung his gear into the back, jumped in, fastened his seatbelt, and started the engine. As he flipped on his flashing emergency lights, he dropped

161

the gear into reverse and was ready to give his truck the gas to back out of the driveway.

Suddenly, a man appeared by his open window. He did a double take. He hadn't seen anybody nearby when he ran to the truck. He didn't even recognize this person even though he knew just about everybody in the small town. He was a complete stranger. The man commanded Lou with authority, "Don't back out! Look behind you first!"

Even though Lou was in a desperate hurry, the urgency of the command demanded that he get out and take a look. As he opened the car door, the man completely disappeared. He had just vanished! Shaking his head, Lou put the truck in park, set the emergency brake, stepped out, and walked behind the truck.

Leaning against the back bumper of the pickup was his little four-year-old neighbor boy sitting on his tricycle and watching the clouds go by, completely oblivious to the world around him!

Lou was later asked, "Who do you think the man was? Where did he come from?"

Without hesitation, Lou responded, "I asked my neighbors about a stranger. Nobody had seen anyone. I just know it was an angel sent in a split-second of time to save a little boy! I'm positive of it, and you'll never convince me otherwise."

See that you do not look down on one of these little ones. For I tell you that their angels in heaven always see he face of my Father in heaven (Matthew 18:10).

FOOD FOR THOUGHT: This portion of Scripture is most often used in making the argument that we all have a guardian angel, especially little children. We can also assume a great number of God's angels are before the Father on duty 24/7 and ready to respond to any command from Him for the care and protection of these little ones.

CHAPTER 52

A LOUD VOICE

*D*ebra Weber of Springfield, Missouri, is a busy lady—she is a mother of three, wife of a busy husband, school teacher and volunteer. She's a woman with lots of things on her mind.

On this particular day, Debra had to run an errand. She was in a hurry and jumped in the car, barreled down the street, and moved into heavier traffic. Then she heard a gentle voice say: "Debra, put on your seatbelt." Although this was her normal routine, she had forgotten to do it when she had started the car, and looking at the cars around her, she didn't think she could take her hands off the wheel to do it now. Busy with watching traffic, she promptly forgot about the command, unusual though the voice was.

About two minutes later the voice came again, this time so loud and so forceful it shook the car: "DEBRA, PUT ON YOUR SEATBELT!"

This time she pulled over and quickly obeyed the voice. She thought, *This is most unusual; where did this voice come from? Am I hearing things or did it really happen?*

Less than five minutes later, as she was moving through a major intersection with the light in her favor, an out-of-control car ran the red light and plowed directly into the passenger side of her car. It demolished her car, but Debra didn't have a scratch on her.

As she related the story to me she asked, "Okay, how do you explain it? I didn't see anything, but I sure heard it."

I had no quick and sure explanation. I just shrugged my shoulders, and she declared, "I believe it was an angel with a loud voice!"

In our last story, there was an appearance in which the angel didn't say a word. But in this story, an angel spoke gently in an audible voice first and then later shouted at her to finally get Debra's attention. How do you explain it?

Do we really need to have a plausible explanation before we become believers? Not everything can be explained by human reasoning. In the spiritual world we are told to be believers and accept some things in faith at face value.

Most of us experience the quiet leading of the Spirit in our lives based on the instructions of God's Word, but at critical times there is a need for the spectacular intervention by angels. Thank God He can work in both ways in our lives!

But after he had considered this, an angel of the Lord appeared to him in a dream and said, "Joseph son of David, do not be afraid to take Mary home as your wife, because what is conceived in her is from the Holy Spirit. She will give birth to a son, and you are to give him the name Jesus, because he will save his people from their sins" (Matthew 1:20-21).

FOOD FOR THOUGHT: There you have it—a biblical setting in which an angel gave specific instructions to Joseph. So why couldn't there be an angel in a car in the twenty-first century? What should the response be to Debra's question? Was it the voice of an angel? Was it a genuine angelic message? How did Joseph know it was an authentic message for his life? How will you know if it's an honest-to-goodness angelic message or some kind of an imaginative fantasy? The simple test is: does it match up with biblical truth?

CHAPTER 53

THE ANGEL PORTER

*H*ere's a story from Cindy and Harold (names changed), a couple who were traveling by train to Mainhausen, Germany.

We knew we had to change trains about midway and take a train going in the opposite direction.

The train station was designed with two sets of tracks and a concrete platform, and another two sets of tracks and then another platform. To get from one platform to the other, you had to go down about twenty-five steps to a concrete corridor or tunnel that went under the tracks and up twenty-five steps to the next platform.

While we were waiting for our next train on the first platform, we looked at the overhead monitor and discovered that we were on the wrong platform. Our train was loading on the next platform, about ready to pull out. We had to quickly move to the next platform to catch the correct train.

Between us we had six heavy suitcases to move. Quickly I grabbed two, about all I could carry, while my wife stayed with the remaining four. I hurried down the steps and struggled up the next set of steps. I dropped the two and turned to go back to the steps to get another two. I needed three trips to carry all six across and prayed I would have enough strength to do this quickly. At the top of the steps going back down, I met a man coming rapidly, almost running and taking two steps at a time, with our four suitcases. He had one under each arm and one in each hand. He walked right by me without a word or nod and set the four down next to the two I had carried.

I looked at my wife, who had followed him, as if to ask, "Who is this?"

In reply, she simply shrugged her shoulders.

When I turned to thank the man, he was gone! Now there were only four other people on this platform with nowhere to go, no place to hide, and no door to quickly duck into. He just vanished!

My wife told me, "All of a sudden he appeared. I hadn't seen him coming. He motioned for me to follow and just picked up the four suitcases as if they had been empty. I just followed him."

I was so surprised that I hadn't taken a close look at him as he came up the stairs with those suitcases. There certainly hadn't appeared to be anything unusual about him. I judged him to be of average size and build. Our suitcases had been packed to the brim with goodies we were taking to friends, as well as our souvenirs. They were heavy—seventy pounds was the limit of weight for our airlines, and they were just at that weight.

I calculated the combined weight of the four suitcases to be more or less about 280 pounds. Now, I don't know very many men who could pick up 280 pounds and run up and down steps with this kind of load. I just don't understand how he could have carried them so quickly or all four at the same time.

The only solution making any sense to us is this must have been some kind of super being. We later concluded during the train ride that this just had to have been an angel to the rescue.

There was a violent earthquake, for an angel of the Lord came down from heaven and, going to the tomb, rolled back the stone and sat on it. His appearance was like lightning, and his clothes were white as snow. The guards were so afraid of him that they shook and became like dead men (Matthew 28:2-4).

FOOD FOR THOUGHT: Can angels do heavy lifting? The biblical account above says an angel rolled back the heavy stone that had been sealed to shut up the tomb of Jesus. So why couldn't an angel carry four heavy suitcases? Isn't it interesting to see the many ways in which angels help out needy folks?

CHAPTER 54

HOW DID HE KNOW?

*H*arold Roberts from Fenton, Missouri, shares with us the next story of angelic help:

We were on a sightseeing tour in the nation of Israel with a group from our church here in Fenton. We were staying in a hotel in the town of Tiberius located on the Sea of Galilee.

After a wonderful Israeli dinner in our hotel dining room, my wife went back to our room, and I told her I'd be back soon and that I was going to take a walk and get some fresh air. Just outside our hotel, I met our guide who engaged me in a bit of conversation. When he asked what my plans were, he offered to give me a ride down to an ice cream parlor a bit more than four blocks away.

After I finished my treat, I decided to walk back to the hotel. I walked four blocks back in the direction of the hotel. Completing the fourth block, I looked for the hotel, but not a sign could be found. By this time it was dark and I kept on walking. Most of the sidewalks were shaded by trees except at the end of each block where there was a street light.

Upon reaching the seventh block with still no hotel in sight, I sensed I was lost. Being in a strange city at night, I looked around for help or at least somebody to ask for directions. There was no one—just darkness—except for the circles of light from the streetlamps at the end of each block. I began to pray and asked the Lord for help.

As I approached the next lighted corner, block number eight by this time, I saw a figure of a man. I couldn't make out his features in the darkness, but I saw his shape. He was looking directly at me. He didn't say anything but motioned for me to follow him. Understandably, I was a bit apprehensive, but then a strange peace and calm seemed to settle over me. This seemed to indicate to me it would be alright to follow him.

He turned to the right, down a narrow dark street and motioned with his right hand for me to follow. He always made sure he kept a certain distance between us. When he came to the end of this block, he crossed the street and stood on the opposite corner under the streetlight and pointed with his hand. I looked in the direction he was pointing and sure enough, there was our hotel! I looked back in his direction to express my thanks, but he was gone! Vanished! I had glanced away not more than two or three seconds. He was simply gone.

By this time, my wife had become alarmed and wondered why I had been gone so long, so she was greatly relieved when she saw me return. I shared with her my little adventure, right down to the details of the strange silent man who gave me directions.

As I have looked back on this experience, I have a number of questions. How did he know I needed help? How did he know what I was attempting to find? How did he know, without asking me, what I needed? How was it possible for him to disappear so quickly? The only logical explanation that satisfies all my questions is I believe with all my heart he was an angel—a silent, quiet angel sent on a mission of mercy.

When the angel of the Lord did not show himself again to Manoah and his wife, Manoah realized that it was the angel of the Lord (Judges 13:21).

FOOD FOR THOUGHT: We have absolutely no way of knowing how many times angels might have been involved in our lives. One might be right at your side, helping you turn the pages of this book. Awesome! Wouldn't it be some kind of an honor? We will never know positively because we understand angels are spirit beings, and most of the time they are invisible. Sometimes angels can show up disguised as ordinary human beings. This is shown often in the Bible as in the case of Manoah and his wife, parents of Samson, when the angel arrived. In fact, they invited him to stay for dinner. Read the story to discover how the angel exited this scene!

CHAPTER 55

HEAVYWEIGHT ANGELS

*M*y mother related this story about another ministry couple who were contemporaries of theirs when they were pastors in Minnesota. The now deceased Pastor and Mrs. B.C. Heinz were the ministry family at a small church in North Dakota.

The Heinzes and another couple from their church made their way to a late springtime fellowship meeting quite a distance away in the town of Dickinson, where Pastor Heinz was to be one of the scheduled speakers. This happened to be one of those all-day affairs—morning service, lunch, afternoon meeting, a minister's business meeting, dinner, and finally the evening rally/service. When it was all finished, it was approximately 10:30 pm as the couple drove away from the church. Springtime weather in North Dakota can be very unpredictable. They turned north on state Highway 85 towards Williston, and about that time it started to rain, sleet, snow, and freeze all at the same time.

They started down into the valley, and the icy mixture soon fell with an even greater intensity. It began to accumulate on the highway, making driving very treacherous and the visibility near zero. They had no snow tires or chains on the car because it was late spring, and they hadn't anticipated any more snow. Mrs. Heinz began to pray: "Help us, Lord, help our car, keep us safe."

As they began the climb from the valley floor, the car began to lose traction and soon they came to a complete stop. No matter what they tried, the car would spin out of control since they had absolutely no traction on the freezing gunk. They could do nothing more than prepare to spend the night huddled in the car, waiting for the snowplow or other help to come their way. The prospect of spending the freezing night in their vehicle was not very pleasant.

About this time a car drove up behind them with six husky young men in it. They stopped behind the stalled car, and one of them asked if they could be of help. Pastor Heinz said, "A push would help us, but what we really need is more traction on the rear end; perhaps more weight would help us make it to the top."

The pastor started the car, and five of these young men began to push the car up the steep snow covered road while the sixth man drove their car behind. As soon as it began rolling, they all jumped up on the trunk. Two were sitting with their feet dangling over the sides and the other three were sitting facing the rear with their feet on the rear bumper. With this help, the car easily made it to the top of the hill.

The pastor immediately stopped the car and got out to thank the kind heavyweight strangers. When he went to speak with them, he discovered that they had all disappeared!

No trace of them nor of their car that had followed them to the top of the hill was visible—not even a tire track!

Billy Graham once wrote: "Reports continually flow to my attention from many places around the world telling of visitors of the angelic order appearing, ministering, fellowshiping, and disappearing."

But you have come to Mount Zion, to the heavenly Jerusalem, the city of the living God. You have come to thousands upon thousands of angels in joyful assembly, to the church of the firstborn, whose names are written in heaven. You have come to God, the judge of all men, to the spirits of righteous men made perfect (Hebrews 12:22-23).

FOOD FOR THOUGHT: Catching a glimpse of angels doesn't depend completely on what form God assigns to them. The Bible strongly supports the concept that the Lord must open our eyes before we can see them. Take the case of Daniel and his companions near the Tigris River: one person saw the angel but the people next to him didn't. Or take the time that a donkey could see the angel, but the person riding the donkey could not.

CHAPTER 56

ANGELS IN THE SNOW

*W*hen you live in Colorado, especially in or near the mountains, or have to cross them in the wintertime, you learn how to travel with provisions such as extra clothing, a survival kit, tire chains, and a snow shovel. What happens when you are caught without these crucial items?

Well, J.D. and his family are native to Colorado and live in Grand Junction on the western slope of the Rocky Mountains. In late August one year, they were returning home from a trip and had to cross Red Mountain Pass from Durango to Grand Junction. It was still summertime, and their car wasn't equipped for winter travel yet. They were making their climb over the pass, which is 11,008 feet in elevation on the top. This highway is named the "Million Dollar Highway" because of the great cost per mile to originally build it. It's one of the most treacherous roads to travel, even in good weather, full of steep grades and hairpin turns but without many guardrails. When the weather is wet, snowy, or icy, the road is downright dangerous and often closed to travel.

J.D.'s family was traveling the road with their three little children. As they neared the top, they noticed a dense cloud cover and a storm brewing, but didn't think too much about it. As they topped out at the summit and started down the other side, they immediately found themselves in a late summer's snowstorm! Wind was blowing the heavy snow, making it freeze to an icy glaze on the roadway. Visibility was poor, but they had no place to turn around or stop. All they could do was to proceed as cautiously as possible in navigating the ice-covered, slick hairpin turns and steep downhill grade. Conditions worsened quickly. The first thing they did was to pray. As J.D. drove, his wife, Agnes, and the kids were praying.

In spite of all J.D.'s careful precautions and downshifting, the car began to slip and slide. The edge of the road, with no guardrail to protect drivers at this stretch, came extremely close. The car continued to skid towards the edge and the hundreds of feet drop to the distant valley below.

All of a sudden, two men appeared running beside the car—one with his hand on the left front fender and the other on the left rear fender. The car straightened out of the skid and these two men continued to run alongside of the car until J.D. had maneuvered it through the last treacherous, icy hairpin curve to enter the town of Ouray.

J.D. pulled the car over to the side of the road and stopped in order to thank the men who had come to their rescue. But as he got out of the car, no one was to be found! There was no place for the men to go but up or down the mountain road, which could clearly be seen in both directions. The family looked but didn't even see any footprints in the snow!

Safely down the mountain, they expressed their thanksgiving to the Lord for His protection and care in sending the two men who had come to their rescue.

Writer and philosopher Joseph Glanvill noted, "What's impossible to all humanity may be possible to the metaphysics and physiology of angels."

The angel of the Lord encamps around those who fear him, and he delivers them (Psalm 34:7).

FOOD FOR THOUGHT: One thing we do know is that angels are God's representatives, messengers ordered by God to help in countless ways. They also protect us in ways we are not aware of. In fact, none of us has any idea of how many times an angel has been there to protect us. Some day in heaven, it will be exciting to see how many times angels were there when we needed them!

CHAPTER 57

A HIGHWAY ANGEL

*V*incent J. Kern of Snellville, Georgia, relates the following experience with an angel:

I'll never forget my encounter with an angel on a Saturday afternoon in mid-October 1979. Through divine intervention, the Lord sent an angel to save my life, an action I still think about now and again, and an encounter for which I shall be eternally grateful.

Due to the responsibilities associated with being an accountant (CPA), it was necessary for my employer to require the entire staff to work a fair amount of overtime during the year in order to meet quarterly and year end tax filing deadlines. After putting in a good fifty-five hours of work for the week, I had decided to call it a day and drive to my home in Wilton, Connecticut. It was a gloomy, wet Saturday afternoon when I proceeded to make the routine half-hour commute back home.

While heading south on the Merritt Parkway, a two-lane highway in southwestern Connecticut, I decided to pass a

179

slow moving vehicle that was traveling a good fifteen miles per hour less than the posted speed limit. I had just gotten parallel with the vehicle I was attempting to pass when my vehicle hit a large puddle forming on the low portion of the highway. Instantly I felt my car losing power and saw several red lights illuminate on my dashboard, indicating my car engine had shut down.

As my powerless Chevy Nova exited this large puddle and started up the next incline, I tried in vain to turn off the highway and park my dying car on the right-hand soft shoulder. Unfortunately, several vehicles in a row wouldn't permit me to pull back into the right lane, leaving me no alternative but to glide to a complete stop in the opposite lane of this two-lane highway.

Realizing the puddle had flooded my car's points and plugs, thereby causing my engine to shut off, I now sat at a complete stop in the left lane of a moderately traveled highway. After I tried unsuccessfully to restart the car, I turned on the four-way flashers and quickly jumped out of the car.

Fearing a possible collision, I stood on the very small left-hand shoulder and motioned for approaching cars to pass my stalled car. Sad to say, when many of the drivers saw me motioning them to move to the right, they decided to shout obscenities at me. After nearly thirty minutes of standing in the lightly falling rain and being maligned by strangers, my car's battery was growing very weak, causing the four-way flashers to cease.

At this point, I observed an older vehicle approaching the rear of my stalled car. I continued to motion the oncoming vehicle to pass, but this vehicle continued to drive directly toward my car. At this point I thought the other car was on a collision course with it, so I jumped over the guardrail to save my life. However, the driver slowed, stopped, rolled down the window, and told me he was going to help me.

As the man walked toward me, I'll never forget his appearance. He was clean shaven, appeared to be in his mid-thirties, with very light blue sparkling eyes, dark blonde hair, and he wore a sport coat. He said to me, "We'll have to get your car over to the right-hand shoulder and out of the way of traffic."

I remember thinking to myself, *Right, Sherlock, how do you think we can push my stalled car up a hill and somehow stop all the oncoming traffic while we accomplish this feat!*

At this point, the clean-shaven man informed me he had a heavy chain in his car, and he would pull me off the road. Within minutes, he pulled his car around mine to the front. He attached the chain and told me to return to my car and successfully pulled my car over to the safety of the highway shoulder on the right side.

It didn't dawn on me until later that the entire time he was helping me, we had encountered no traffic coming from either direction! This was highly unlikely. Unusual, maybe even impossible!

Out of harm's way, he removed the chain. I attempted to start the car once more, but it was hopeless. He asked, "Is there anything else I can do to help you?"

"Yes," I replied. "Would you please drive me to the next exit so I could phone a friend who might be home so he could come and pick me up?" He obliged and within a couple of minutes we pulled up at a phone booth not far from the exit ramp.

As I was about to get out of his car, I noticed my new-found friend was soaking wet, and his sport coat was a mess. I insisted that he should take a twenty dollar bill at the least to cover the cost of dry-cleaning his coat. Three times I insisted, and each time he refused my small reward. I'll never forget the odd look on his face after rejecting my third offer for the money.

He looked directly at me with those piercing blue eyes as though he were looking right through me and said, "Don't thank me for being here; thank God for sending me to you."

His words caught me off guard, yet I knew he meant every word of it. With that I got out of the car and watched as he drove away—he and the car simply vanished. Gone. I could see down the highway about two or three miles, but he was long gone before he should have even reached the next curve.

I phoned my friend, and he arrived shortly and drove us back to the stalled car. As he drove I briefly explained the afternoon's encounter, and he listened intently. At the disabled car, I figured I would make one final attempt to start it. When I opened the driver's door, I noticed the interior dome light was brightly lit. I turned the key in the ignition, and it immediately started. I glanced at the gauge on the dash to discover the previously dead battery was now fully charged! I had worked on a number of cars in the past and knew this was far from normal.

The story doesn't end here. During the next ten years I retold this story a handful of times to friends. Eight years later I sold my CPA practice and accepted a professional position in the Atlanta, Georgia, area.

Shortly afterwards, I attended a church conference.

While I was there, a middle-aged African-American walked up to me, looked me in the eye, and told me that there were three separate times in my life when the Lord had sent angels to protect me from imminent death by putting His hand of divine protection upon me.

Then he began to laugh! He continued, "The man who so graciously rescued you on the highway was an angel sent by God, and both God and the angel found it humorous when you attempted to offer an angel twenty dollars for his sport coat to be cleaned!"

Then this African-American disappeared. Since I had never seen him before and wanted to track him down to thank him for those words, I inquired about him. It turned out that no one knew him, or had seen him, or even knew where he could have come from!

I consider this to have been a direct confirmation from the Lord as to His divine intervention on my behalf. And He just might have sent another angel to share the message with me!

He holds victory in store for the upright, he is a shield to those whose walk is blameless, for he guards the course of the just and protects the way of his faithful ones (Proverbs 2:7-8).

FOOD FOR THOUGHT: What an amazing story! It's the last part that makes it different from many of the others we have read about help and deliverance. What a wonderful God! What a caring God who can and will send an angel to "guard the course of the just and protect the way" of His followers! What a word of assurance!

BLESSINGS AND ENCOURAGEMENT

An angel from heaven appeared to him and strengthened him (Luke 22:43).

CHAPTER 58

JUST TO TALK

*C*ora was in her late eighties, and age and time had taken its toll on her body. Although she was confined to a bed due to her physical limitations, her attitude and spirit were still very strong.

She was an avid reader of her Bible and would sing songs as long as her strength and days would allow. When the pain became too great, like most of us, she sometimes became a bit depressed and began to question her situation. Many times she would pray and ask the Lord how long until she would be taken out of this world. She wondered why she was still being left in the world to suffer.

Even when she was depressed, though, her smile never left her; she still would sing her songs and be vibrant. She prayed and asked God for a specific sign about His loving care. Did He still know where she was? Did He still care about her?

One evening when she was alone in her room and could not sleep, suddenly a bright light filled the room. Something she had only read about unfolded before her eyes.

An angel came into the room and stood by her bedside table and smiled at Cora! She later said, "I knew it was an angel because of the way he looked. There was something special about him and his presence. I have never felt such peace come over me." When Cora later told the story, her face lit up with excitement.

Then the angel began to speak softly, in a soothing manner, and assured her of God's love and faithfulness to her. He told her that God knew exactly where she was, and He would be with her every day of her life. He said God knew all about her weakened condition, but she should never be fearful again. He explained that her pain and difficulties would soon be over, and she would be taken home to her final place of rest and peace.

Later she remembered looking at her clock both before and after the angelic visit and determined the angel stayed for about fifteen minutes and then walked through the wall and disappeared.

On the evening of that first day of the week, when the disciples were together, with the doors locked for fear of the Jews, Jesus came and stood among them and said, "Peace be with you!" (John 20:19).

FOOD FOR THOUGHT: Each one who has had an angelic encounter always seems to remark about the peace that surrounds these events. And when angels speak, they always direct praise to their heavenly Father who sent them. Angels are not to be worshiped; only God is worthy to be praised. If we need help, we direct our prayers to God who may choose to send an angel in answer to that prayer.

CHAPTER 59

AN ANGEL NAMED SAMUEL

*C*andy wrote the following story for me to share with you.

One hot summer night my husband, our son, his friend, and I were in our van driving home. We spotted a Dairy Queen, though not in the best part of town. We pooled our pocked money together and discovered we had enough for small cones for each of us, so we stopped to get them.

My husband gathered the coins and went to the window where he stood third in line. We felt a bump against the side of the van and our son said, "Check out this guy that just bumped us, Mom. He looks like he's drunk." He moved toward the front passenger's side window where I could see him. Indeed, he appeared unstable. He was a tall, elderly black man with a patch over his left eye.

As new Christians, I just knew my husband would have to do something for this man, but I was apprehensive about him doing so. We were in a bad part of town where we knew no one, and the man looked ominous. Sure enough, my husband looked back, saw the man, returned to the van, and said to him, "You don't need ice cream—you need some food."

Another fast food restaurant was located just across the street. My husband helped the man into our van and drove there. He bought a small hamburger and a cup of coffee, all that he could afford to buy. As we handed him the food, something strange happened—our stranger was suddenly sober! He began talking about God. He shared things about God that only a Bible scholar would know or at least someone who knew God quite well. He told us about God's creation, a butterfly's wing, a bird's feather, a flower petal, and a newborn baby. He quoted Scripture for us. We were amazed and transfixed.

Then we attempted to find a place for him to stay the night, and it soon dawned on us that this would not be easy. The YMCA, the Salvation Army, and the mission were all closed. The hour was late, and we had no money for a hotel. We were familiar with the town, as we had previously lived there. No luck, no accommodations. All the while, the man continued to tell us about the Lord. After about forty-five minutes of fruitlessly searching for a place for him to stay, he said to us, "Take me back to where you found me. Someone is waiting for me there."

My husband and I looked at each other and both knew what the other was thinking: *Why in the world didn't he tell us this before we had spent a good part of the night looking for a place for him?* My husband turned the van around and drove back to the ice cream place.

The Dairy Queen was now closed, the lights were off, and the parking lot was empty. Where was this person who was waiting for our passenger? Even though no one was in

189

sight, the man said it was okay to let him out of the van. He walked up to my window, looked at me, and said, "You are a new Christian. Will you pray for me?" I was so shocked. How could he have known this? We hadn't told him. I did pray for him and when I finished, I looked at him again. His only visible eye looked as soft as a marshmallow as though I could look into his soul. He smiled, took a step back, and said the strangest thing: "Remember, my name is Samuel, just Samuel."

As we prepared to pull away, all of us looked toward the street to see if any cars were coming. When we looked back to say goodbye, he was gone. The parking lot was rather large and open. Nothing and no one were in sight. Our son jumped out to check to see if possibly he could have fallen. Just like that, he had vanished.

All I could think of was to get home so I could check what he had said and perhaps I could get some answers. I turned to Hebrews 13:2 where it talks about entertaining angels. As I read, the Scripture said, "I will send you My angel, his name is Samuel, and he will tell you of many wonderful things." Later I tried to find this particular sentence again but to no avail. Did God place it there just for me for this moment in time and later erase it from my Bible? I couldn't sleep that night for the excitement.

The next day was Sunday. I don't think you'll be surprised to know that the pastor's sermon text came from Hebrews 13:2. We concluded that we had met and entertained one of God's angels named Samuel!

Keep on loving each other as brothers [sisters]. Do not forget to entertain strangers, for by so doing some people have entertained angels without knowing it (Hebrews 13:1-2).

FOOD FOR THOUGHT: Could this have been a test to see if this family truly would be willing to entertain a stranger in need? Candy later related, "If it had not been for my husband, I might have missed out on this test because of my fears. It has been one of the highlights of my Christian life." It's possible to entertain angels and not even know it. According to Candy, "Yes, there are angels, and one of them is named Samuel!"

CHAPTER 60

THE BLESSING ANGEL

*T*ammy shares with us an unforgettable experience her family had with an angel that forever changed their future.

Driving home from work one Sunday morning, my uncle saw a man walking down the side of Interstate 70, carrying a large old suitcase. It's very unusual to see a hitchhiker on the interstate, and my uncle was not in the habit of picking them up. But he felt compelled to stop for this white-headed, elderly gentleman. My uncle asked him where he was going, and the man replied, "Illinois."

My uncle wasn't going that far because he lived in Elkland, Missouri. However, he invited the man for dinner at my grandmother's house and assured him he'd bring him back to the highway later where he could catch a ride to Illinois. Each Sunday the whole family always gathered at Grandma's for dinner. Afterwards the man went with my uncle to a special service in a nearby town and brought him to our house to spend the night. We lived in a little old house with only two bedrooms. My parents shared a room and my three siblings and I (all small children at the time) shared the other. It was tight quarters, but we made it work.

My parents said an unexplainable feeling of peace surrounded this man. He spoke with such wisdom and gentleness. My mom said, "It just brought goose bumps upon goose bumps just to be near him."

Before my uncle returned with this guest, two of my brothers got into a fight and accidentally knocked the old suitcase off the edge of the bed onto the floor. As it hit the floor, the lid popped open and revealed one item—a very large, worn, old Bible.

When my uncle returned with this guest later that night, we all sat and visited with this man. We were mesmerized. My dad asked questions, and this man would speak to God as if God were sitting right there beside us, and then answer Dad. While he was speaking with us, we felt an overwhelming powerful presence in the room.

The next morning we were all up early and found this man blessing our house. He blessed every room in our humble home. Then he blessed each of us kids individually; he blessed my parents; he even blessed our old worn out car.

My dad drove him to the bus station and bought him a ticket to Illinois. We didn't have much to give, but Dad had taught us to be givers, and he set the example. After buying the ticket, Dad pulled out his wallet and gave the man everything he had left—a total of about eighty dollars, which was a huge sum for us. At this time Dad was a truck driver and had to be gone much of the time so Mom took care of us four kids and was unable to work.

Dad thought all the way home, *How am I going to feed my family this week? That was all of our grocery money.*

Later that afternoon a check arrived in the mail for more than two hundred dollars from a totally unexpected source. From that point on, circumstances changed for our family. Dad kept on getting better and better jobs. We were able to move into bigger houses and drove nicer and newer cars. Our family was even healthier. We were amazed at how things improved after this special visitor had been our guest. The little old house he had blessed was later turned into a church where I became a Christian.

From that time of blessing, my parents, my brothers, my sisters, and all of our families are living for the Lord, and all are using our talents to glorify God. All of these blessings can be traced to the stranger who stayed a night with us. We are absolutely convinced that it was an angel who came to visit and bless us.

And again, when God brings his firstborn into the world, he says, "Let all God's angels worship him." In speaking of the angels he says, "He makes his angels winds, his servants flames of fire" (Hebrews 1:6-7).

FOOD FOR THOUGHT: Here is an instance of an angelic visit witnessed and experienced by an entire family that has received long-term benefits. Even today, this family continues to be blessed.

CHAPTER 61

LEGIONS OF ANGELS

*S*teven N. Crino, of Marshfield, Missouri, had an experience with angels that he will never forget. In the fall of 1981, his best friend's mother and his brother led him to know Christ. It was clear to Steve that they had experienced God in a way he had never known. They warned him that once a person receives Christ, he may enter into a very real spiritual war. They further explained to him that he could expect some kind of attempt to lure him back into his old lifestyle.

Let's let Steve tell it in his own words:

Shortly after I came to know Christ, I was asked to house-sit at my sister's home and care for their family dog while they vacationed. They had a large, beautiful, two-story Cape Cod styled home not far from the Atlantic Ocean. Could this be the time and place for a spiritual battle?

I worked during part of the day and also attended classes at the state junior college. On this particular night I was studying at the kitchen table in my sister's home. Suddenly I had a sense of terror so intense that I was afraid to even lift my gaze from my studies, convinced I would see something demonic if I did. I know of no other way to describe it than an overwhelming fear and a sense that I was in the presence of something or someone I did not care to see!

I got on the phone and tried to contact my friend's mother to ask her to pray for me. She was busy, so I told my friend the situation and asked him to tell his mother so she would pray for me. As a new believer, I felt she had more influence with God than I did. Still consumed with fear, I went back to my studies.

All of a sudden, a peace washed over me like I had never known or even heard of before, and every trace of fear evaporated. It was instantaneous and the contrast between the way I felt just moments earlier and the peace that now consumed me was positively amazing!

Not understanding such things, I just simply lifted my gaze towards heaven and said, "I don't know what this is, but thank you, Lord!" I saw the clock on the wall reading 9:45 p.m. and made a mental note of it.

After my studies I took the dog out and when he came back in, I headed up for bed. As I walked through the dining room and up the stairs, I began to sense a heavenly presence that I will never forget. As I climbed the stairs, this sense grew more intense. As I reached the bedroom it grew more intense! With all the partying I had done in the years before, I had experienced many kinds of earthly "highs," but this experience was so far beyond that and so much better, it was like comparing heaven with hell. This peaceful presence was incredible. I could not believe that the God of all the galaxies cared enough to touch such a wretched specimen as me in this way!

I thanked God over and over again through my tears of joy. The room was filled with a glow and warmth that was indescribable. I couldn't make out distinct figures, but a general glow, a three-dimension kind of thing was present. I just knew something or someone was there.

I eventually fell into the best sleep of my life. My soul felt cleansed; my body felt renewed; my mind was refreshed. It was amazing.

The next day I called my best friend's mother and asked her if she had been praying for me. She said she had prayed that God would surround my bed with a legion of angels, and that He would allow me to feel their presence. (A legion is between three and six thousand!) All I know is that there was an eternal kind of happening. I then asked her about the time she had prayed, and she said that it was 9:45!

More than twenty years have come and gone since that incredible night, but I have never forgotten the wonder and awe of that experience. I can hardly wait to meet the Lord and those mighty angels in heaven one day.

But you have come to Mount Zion, to the heavenly Jerusalem, the city of the living God. You have come to thousands upon thousands of angels in joyful assembly, to the church of the firstborn, whose names are written in heaven. You have come to God (Hebrews 12:22-23).

FOOD FOR THOUGHT: It doesn't seem that you must always see an angel to sense their presence. In the above illustration no angels appeared distinctively, yet this young man sensed their presence and experienced something beyond description. Perhaps you've never seen an angel, but you have known their presence!

CHAPTER 62

HEAVENLY PHONE SYSTEM

One Saturday night, a pastor of a church was working late in his office making some last minute preparations for the services on Sunday. It was almost 10:00 p.m. when he decided to call his wife before he left for home. He called her but she didn't answer, so he let it ring and ring. He was puzzled and thought it very odd that she didn't answer. He wrapped up a few more things and then called her again.

This time she answered immediately. He asked her why she hadn't answered the phone when he called before. She replied, "The phone hasn't rung any other time this night. I've been home all night, and this is the first time it has rung." He brushed it off as a fluke and made his way home.

Two days later, the pastor was in his office again when he received a very strange call. It was from a man who wanted to know why the pastor had called him on the previous Saturday night.

The pastor said, "I don't know what you are talking about. I only made one call that night. I didn't call you; I'm sorry."

This man replied, "My phone rang and rang for about twelve rings, but I didn't answer."

The pastor suddenly realized what had happened and apologized for disturbing the man. He explained that the call had been to his wife at home that night. "Perhaps I misdialed and got the wrong number."

The man responded, "That's quite all right. Let me tell you my story. You see, I was planning to commit suicide on Saturday night and was ready to end my life, but before I did, I prayed, 'God, if You're up there and You don't want me to do this thing, give me a sign NOW!' At that very point my phone began to ring. And it kept on ringing until I went and looked at the caller ID. It said, ALMIGHTY GOD, and I was afraid to pick up the phone to answer Almighty God, so I just let it ring."

The pastor then said, "The reason it showed that on your caller ID is that I pastor a church named 'ALMIGHTY GOD TABERNACLE'!"

The man was overwhelmed and the pastor prayed with him, and later counseled him and helped him get his life back on track.

Now, we don't know what happened that night. Did the pastor misdial a number that was quite different from his home number? Or did God just take that signal and send it to the man in need? Did an angel get into the phone works and reroute this signal? We don't know, but we do know that on that particular night at that particular moment, a needy man experienced a revelation of the love of God in a spectacular way with spectacular timing!

Then Nebuchadnezzar said, "Praise be to the God of Shadrach, Meshach and Abednego, who has sent his angel and rescued his servants!" (Daniel 3:28).

FOOD FOR THOUGHT: Okay...what about you and me? As we walk our daily walk and carry out our life here in our communities, it is important to realize that our relationship with God must have first priority. And in that relationship we must also realize God really cares for each of us and knows where we are and the difficulties we may be facing. What a comfort!

CHAPTER 63

BE PREPARED

*J*ack Tibbitts of Meadow Lakes, Texas, hadn't thought of it in terms of angels speaking to him, but God entered his life in a very real way. It happened when his children were small, and he was working as a salesman for General Electric in Dayton, Ohio. He had grown up on a farm in a rural area 30 miles from La Crosse, Wisconsin, and their church was a Presbyterian church in nearby North Bend.

Here's Jack's story:

One day I had the strangest feeling. It was a crystal clear thought, as distinct as if a voice told me I was supposed to prepare to preach a sermon in the North Bend church where I had grown up and attended church. Speaking from the pulpit was one of the very last things in the world I would have felt comfortable doing, and I attempted to shove it out of my mind. But the message was repeated. I ignored it…it couldn't be possible that I was supposed to take this bold step. When the message came again, I was told to use John 15:13 as a basis for what I was supposed to teach. Now this was really odd because I had never spoken in a church before, let alone behind the pulpit! Specifically the text said, "Greater love has no man than this, that he should lay down his life for his friends." I was to speak about laying down my life in a spiritual sense. I interpreted it to mean I was supposed to witness to what Jesus Christ meant in my life.

Writing out any talk was difficult for me, but I said, "Okay, Lord," and prepared. When finished, I asked, "What should I do now, Lord?" This happened in the middle of May, and the instructions distinctively came in a clear voice to go to my parents' home in North Bend over the Memorial Day weekend. This trip entailed driving 600 miles up on Saturday and back on Monday with four children under seven years of age. This was before the days of interstate highways, and I thought my wife, Helen, would think I was crazy (I hadn't told her of the messages I had been getting). But she agreed we should go.

We arrived at my parents' home on Saturday evening, but I didn't have the courage to tell them the real reason why we were there. Instead I asked, "Who is preaching tomorrow at church?" My mother replied the regular pastor had been called to another church and seminary students from Dubuque Seminary were filling the pulpit. I still said nothing, and we all went to church the next morning.

As we walked in the door, an old neighbor greeted us warmly but then said, "It is too bad you came today; we may not have a minister. Our supply pastor hasn't shown up. This has never happened before."

Somehow, this didn't surprise me, but I was too shy to say, "I am all ready if you want me to preach." Instead, I thought to myself, *Okay Lord, You have gotten me this far, You tell them,* so I just went in and took a seat with the family.

The elders of the church quickly met in the narthex to decide what to do, and they decided to have my mother lead the service but omit the sermon. I happened to be sitting on the aisle as my mother went up to start the service. As she passed me, she leaned over and asked if there was anything I could possibly say. I replied, "Yes, I would be glad to."

I gave the sermon I had prepared and used the notes without any trepidation and with a tremendous sense of fulfillment. I don't know if it had any impact on anyone else, but it sure was a mountain top experience for me!

God will order his angels to take good care of you (Luke 4:10 TEV).

FOOD FOR THOUGHT: Are you thinking, "But

where were the angels in Jack Tibbitt's story?" He hadn't really seen any, but as he has reflected on this over the years, he's concluded that it was angels at work on God's behalf. You don't have to see angels to know that angels are at work. As you study them from the Bible, one thing stands out: angels are not looking for publicity or visibility. Apparently all they have in mind, when on a mission, is to get their job done. Often, they can be at work completely behind the scenes, but sometimes so near we can almost feel their breath (if they do have breath).

CHAPTER 64

EVER ENTERTAINED ANGELS?

*G*ene and Judy lived in a southern state and were the parents of six kids ranging in age from five to fifteen. They were a church-going, church-loving family. Gene had worked at the local lumber mill for a number of years; when it folded, he was left with nothing but odd jobs to make a living.

One day he had a small job in town repairing a car. On this day Judy was doing the laundry and had invited some church ladies over for an afternoon coffee. Their conversation was broken when Judy's oldest came running into the house.

"Mom," she said, "there's a man coming around to the back door. Says he's got to talk to you."

Immediately these well-meaning church ladies warned, "Be careful. Don't have anythin' to do with a man who's comin' beggin'! Now hear!"

At the back door stood an elderly African-American with graying hair and soft, warm eyes.

"Ma'am," he said, "sorry to bother you, but my truck broke down, and I'm walking to town. I would appreciate it if you could give me some water and a bit of food if you could spare it."

Judy was stunned. She found herself hesitant to do the right thing because she had been influenced by the ladies. Instead of getting the water and food she stood there. Their eyes met and the old man waited a few seconds and then silently turned away. Judy felt ashamed as she went back to the table, but even worse was the condemning look she received from her oldest daughter.

Quickly she grabbed a pitcher of lemonade and some cookies and ran out the front door to find the old man on his knees with the rest of the children around him listening as he was telling them a Bible story. She offered the cookies and lemonade and told him to wait as she went back in the house to prepare a sack lunch for him. She returned and said, "I'm sorry about the way I acted."

"That's all right," he said. "Too many people are influenced by others. But unlike some, you have overcome it. This speaks well for you."

That night Gene had wonderful news! The car he had repaired belonged to a man whose brother ran a repair shop and happened to be looking for a good mechanic. He hired Gene on the spot!

Later, Judy told Gene about the events of the afternoon. When she was finished, he asked, "Did you say this was an elderly black man? Kind-looking eyes and gray hair?" He jumped out of bed and went through his pockets until he found a piece of folded paper that he handed to Judy.

He said, "I met that man walking down the road when I came from town. He waved me over and gave this to me. I took the note and quickly read it. When I looked up, he was gone! Just disappeared! I got out of the car and looked up and down the road. I could see for a good mile or more in each direction, but he was gone! I thought it strange but haven't had time to think any more about it."

Judy unfolded the note and began to cry as she read it. Here's what it said: "Do not forget to entertain strangers, for by so doing some people have entertained angels without knowing it."

Keep on loving each other as brothers [and sisters]. *Do not forget to entertain strangers, for by so doing some people have entertained angels without knowing it. Remember those in prison as if you were their fellow prisoners, and those who are mistreated as if you yourselves were suffering* (Hebrews 13:1-3).

FOOD FOR THOUGHT: How many strangers have you entertained that in reality were angels? In today's world we are always cautioned about strangers and told to avoid them. But does that make it right? We need to be careful, yes. But if and when you do open your heart to strangers, you might be having a wonderful adventure. Who knows?

CHAPTER 65

IS IT REALLY AN ANGEL?

*L*ee McGinnis of Branson West, Missouri, was unemployed and discouraged. A split second encounter with an angel gave him just the encouragement he needed. Lee tells his story:

At that time, I was unemployed after having worked some thirty years in the same occupation. We were living on my wife's salary that she earned at a local college. This was a tough time financially for us. I had sent out resumes but didn't get the answers I had hoped for.

One day in August I went to the mailbox looking for something, just anything by way of an answer or encouragement. The only thing in the box was an advertising flyer for back-to-school clothes for kids. By this time our kids had all left home, married, and were having kids of their own. On the way back to the house from the mailbox, about halfway up the driveway, I became overwhelmed with discouragement and stopped and looked at the flyer again. With tears in my eyes I complained, "Lord, I don't even have any kids going back to school."

At this moment in time, a young man came down the street riding a bicycle. He was dressed in bike riding gear and looked about as normal as he could be. I didn't pay too much attention to him until he shouted at me, "Jesus! Look to the Lord, Bud!" That's all he said, and it took me by surprise. I turned to get a look at who he was and where he was going, but he had vanished! I could see down the road a good half mile or more, and he was out of sight! He had disappeared as I watched!

What do you think? Lee McGinnis said, "I saw an angel riding a bicycle. I believe I did to this day. It was just another way for God to lift my spirits and help me to look to Him for strength and guidance."

How can you be sure if you sense or see what you think might be an angel? We again refer to the Bible for the real answers. When the angel Gabriel came to Daniel, he told him, "Therefore consider the message, and understand the revelation." Daniel, sure enough, saw the angel and heard him, but he was still required to use his own thinking powers in evaluating what the angel had told him.

This should be one of God's concepts for us in regards to what may happen in an angelic encounter. The first consideration is to regard what the Bible has to say about angels and their ministry. And the second is to place it into context with our own life experiences.

Have you been doing this as you are reading through this book? Are you really looking over these angelic encounters with your mind and with your knowledge of the Bible?

Are you prepared to do this if and when you might encounter the presence of a totally spiritual being? The Bible is also clear that we are to "test the spirits" according to the apostle John in 1 John 4:1-3.

Dear friends, do not believe every spirit, but test the spirits to see whether they are from God, because many false prophets have gone out into the world. This is how you can recognize the Spirit of God: Every spirit that acknowledges that Jesus Christ has come in the flesh is from God, but every spirit that does not acknowledge Jesus is not from God. This is the spirit of the antichrist, which you have heard is coming and even now is already in the world.

And angels are spirits! The apostle Paul confers with this thinking also. "Test everything. Hold on to the good. Avoid every kind of evil" (1 Thessalonians 5:21-22).

The best test is to keep Jesus Christ front and center in your mind, soul, and spirit.

Now let me pose this question to you: What would excite you most—God's message to you or getting to see an angel?

Praise the Lord, you his angels, you mighty ones who do his bidding, who obey his word. Praise the Lord, all his heavenly hosts, you his servants who do his will. Praise the Lord, all his works everywhere in his dominion. Praise the Lord, O my soul (Psalm 103:20-22).

FOOD FOR THOUGHT: There is an observation I'm quite sure you will have to agree with: Those people in the Bible who were given the privilege of a direct visible or spoken ministry from angels are those with a mature enough spiritual attitude to want an encounter with God, not with angels. For example, Mary had a conversation with two at the empty tomb of Jesus, but when she returned to tell the disciples, she didn't say, "I have seen two angels." She said, "I have seen the Lord!" Her heart, life, mind, perspective, and spirit were right, so God was able to allow her to see angels.

CHAPTER 66

ANGELS ON VIGIL

*T*his story comes to us from Misty Isaacs, of Kingsport, Tennessee, and concerns her mother, Velma Ezell, Velma's identical twin sister, Melba McCroskey, and Melba's daughter, Cindy Stafford.

Shortly after Cindy married, Melba was diagnosed with "amyotrophic lateral sclerosis" (ALS or Lou Gehrig's disease), which attacks and destroys muscles and nerves although the mind is not affected. Her disease progressed rapidly and she was soon confined to a wheelchair and attached to an oxygen machine. She lived in this state for three years and never complained, but often spent her time in prayer for her lost friends and family. She had a sharp mind and a wonderful, uplifting attitude.

Soon she only had the use of her eyes, but could those eyes ever talk! A communication method was worked out so she could spell words with her eyes in which she would close her eyes for "no" and raise her eyebrows for "yes." When she needed to emphasize, she managed to utter a groan along with her eye motions. The system worked well because her twin sister was really able to anticipate what was in her mind because they had the unique connection that twins often do. Let's let Misty tell the story:

My mother, Velma, and my cousin Cindy took turns keeping vigil by my Aunt Melba's bedside. We all knew the end was nearing when the family was called one day. Velma was alone in the room with Melba as the doctor broke the news. Velma closed her eyes and began to cry and pray while holding Melba's hand. Suddenly she felt a substantial hand placed on her shoulder, obviously for comfort. Her assumption was that it was the hand of the doctor, but when she opened her eyes to acknowledge him, she saw that he was not in the room. She felt chills and turned back to her sister whose eyes were wide open.

Velma told the sick woman about the hand and asked Melba if it was the doctor. Melba closed her eyes for "no!"

Then Velma asked, "Was it an angel?" Melba emphatically raised her eyebrows and let out a groan. She flashed her eyes around the room.

Velma asked if they were with her all the time, and she answered with an emphatic "yes!" Then she communicated that she saw them every day around her bed!

She didn't die that night but lived a little over a month longer until the first day of spring. It was just long enough for her daughter, Cindy, to have her own personal angelic visit. Cindy was in the kitchen and was passing Melba's room to go the den. (Melba lived out her illness at home, and all these visits took place in her bedroom.) From the corner of her eye she saw someone standing at the foot of her mother's bed. She passed by again but did not see the figure. Cindy then told her mother that she had seen someone at the foot of her bed, and Melba acknowledged with the familiar eyebrow and groan, "yes!" Cindy questioned the sick woman further, asking her if this was an angel, and she received another emphatic "yes." She again flashed those eyes around the room to let Cindy know that her room was full of them day and night.

Visitors and other family members didn't see any of the angels mentioned above, but they all had the sense of being in the presence of something or someone very holy and awesome. What a source of encouragement to know that in this time of need the angels stood vigil until it was time to take Melba to her heavenly home.

After the Lord Jesus had spoken to them, he was taken up into heaven and he sat at the right hand of God (Mark 16:19).

While he was blessing them, he left them and was taken up into heaven (Luke 24:51).

FOOD FOR THOUGHT: Angels were present to give comfort when Melba's physical body let her down. They offered strength when her body had forsaken her. They provided peace and consolation to those who loved her. This was a glimpse of the tender side of God who sent a host of angels to cradle His child until it was time for her to be with Him.

CHAPTER 67

MYSTERIOUS GRANDSONS

This is another angel story that has taken on a life of its own like an urban legend. I have heard a number of versions in a number of different settings and locations, but all contain the same elements. So, let's share the story set in Chicago. What makes this story different is the proof supposedly is still evident to this day, if you know where to look. Don't miss the ending! The story goes like this:

The story took place in the 1870s. It supposedly involved a priest, Arnold Damen and the Society of Jesus. He is the priest who purportedly founded an "altar-boy" society. He taught many young boys the tradition of the Mass and how they were to assist the priest with their duties.

Years of faithful service passed and finally Father Damen went into retirement. He ministered only on special occasions and served as a mentor to young priests.

One dark, stormy night, the doorbell rang at the rectory and the young assistant answered the door to find two young boys on the steps. They explained their grandmother was really sick, and she was in need of a priest because she would not last through the night.

The assistant said, "It's too cold and rainy tonight, boys. I'll make sure to send a priest tomorrow."

But behind the assistant stood the retired old priest listening to the conversation. Father Damen went to the door and told the boys, "I'll come right now. Come in to warm yourself while I get ready."

Not long afterwards, the two boys led the priest through the deserted wet streets until they came to an old apartment house about a mile from the rectory. The boys pointed to a window on the top story of the old building and told him he would find their grandmother there.

The priest went into the building, but the boys didn't follow. He climbed the narrow winding staircase and found the door open. He gently knocked and entered to find an elderly woman. She was cold, very sick and seemed close to death. He ministered to her and gave her communion.

"Father," she managed to whisper, "how did you happen to come here? Some people in the building know I'm sick, but none of them are Catholic."

He stared at her strangely and then said, "Your two grandsons came for me and I followed them here. They told me you could be found in this apartment."

She closed her eyes and with a smile said, "Father, I had two grandsons and they were altar boys at Holy Family Church, but they both died years ago."

Here's the clincher! I've been told the Holy Family Church still stands just west of the University of Illinois' Circle Campus on Roosevelt Road. And further, I've been told that if you visit the sanctuary, high over the entrance you will see the statues of two altar boys, one on each side, holding candles while they face each other. Supposedly these statues were commissioned by Father Damen in honor of what he had considered to have been the visit of two angels disguised as altar boys one cold, dark, rainy night in Chicago in the 1870s.

Suddenly an angel of the Lord appeared and a light shone in the cell. He struck Peter on the side and woke him up. "Quick, get up!" he said, and the chains fell off Peter's wrists. Then the angel said to him, "Put on your clothes and sandals." And Peter did so. "Wrap your cloak around you and follow me," the angel told him. Peter followed him out of the prison, but he had no idea that what the angel was doing was really happening" (Acts 12:7-9).

FOOD FOR THOUGHT: In the story, did some architect originally plan the statues of the altar boys and the story has been told to fit the statues or the other way around, as in the story? Whatever, it's a great story. And in the Bible, many of the angel occurrences involve an action, such as in the angel who commanded Peter to get dressed and follow him.

CHAPTER 68

ANGELS IN MEN'S CLOTHING

*H*enrietta W. Romman of Rogersville, Missouri, shares another of her experiences with us:

I shall tell you about a very recent encounter with angels in human form, dressed in modern clothes and behaving like most of us do.

We were among the crowds of people heading to their seats on September 13, 2003 in the Hammons Student Center auditorium, located on the campus of Southwest Missouri State University in Springfield, Missouri. This event occurred on the second day of the convention of a well-known evangelist.

My husband William and I had been quite positive such services were not for us, yet it had been arranged for us to attend. We felt our assignment was to do more than attend; we were to be in prayer for others who were in attendance.

When we arrived in the early afternoon, it was as though our seats had already been reserved for us. The ushers seated us on the first and only two seats available in a section.

Immediately in front of us was an aisle about five yards wide. These happened to be the best seats in the house, and we could easily take in all the action.

After we sat down, William and I bent our heads and held hands as we began to pray for people who would be in need. After a bit, we opened our eyes and watched. Lots of people came by, all with something in their hands such as something to drink or something to munch on—all except three young men who approached us empty-handed. The first one smiled beautifully at us. He was extremely tall, with blond hair and deep green eyes. I noticed his clothing—a blue shirt, denim jeans, and a denim jacket casually thrown over his left shoulder.

They came closer and the first one knelt on one knee so as to be at eye level with us. He reached out his hand and first greeted William and then held my hand. (It seemed as though this was happening away from the hustle and bustle of the auditorium; it was so quiet and peaceful.) He looked at us from one to the other. It was so strange. I attempted to introduce ourselves. He abruptly cut me short and exclaimed: "We know you! We want you to know that God loves you. God appreciates you. Your prayers are always heard. Listen! We are here to tell you that you are doing well in teaching the young people around you to be good apostles. But you both are meeting with much spiritual warfare. Please look at the Word of God and carry on. Don't be afraid. Take heart in your work!"

Then he stood up. We stood up, and I almost shrieked at him, "What is your name?"

He looked as if searching for a name to end this encounter. Twice he uttered, "Steven, Steven."

Then with those same beautiful smiles, the three visitors continued on their way and swept past us. We keenly watched them for a second or two, and then they quietly melted into thin air!

We looked at each other with our hearts beating fast. Our spirits were enriched and inspired. We looked around and asked the folks sitting next to us if they had just seen our three visitors. It turned out that no one else had seen them.

Then and there, because I am a writer and a columnist, I took out my notebook and wrote down every single word of the one-way communication from God's messengers sent to us. Then, once more, together we bowed our heads reverently and prayed, "Thank You, Lord. Thank You for trusting us."

When I was a child, I talked like a child, I thought like a child, I reasoned like a child. When I became a man I put childish ways behind me. Now we see but a poor reflection in a mirror; then we shall see face to face. Now I know in part; then I shall know fully, even as I am fully known (1 Corinthians 13:11-12).

FOOD FOR THOUGHT: Angels are sent to minister to us personally! Many biblical accounts assure us that we are the objects of their personal concern. Martin Luther wrote the book, *Table Talk,* and in it makes this statement: "An angel is a spiritual creature created by God without a body, for the service of Christendom and the church."

CHAPTER 69

THE "TEST" ANGEL

*T*he next story was given to me by Sara Shockley, from Lawson, Missouri.

One day not long ago, I was driving down the road on my way to Wal-Mart. There was nothing special about the day...nothing special about what I was doing, just a very ordinary day. I was definitely not expecting anything different to happen.

As I was driving, I noticed a shabbily clothed man with a backpack walking on the shoulder of the blacktop in the same direction I was traveling. He was not acting like a hitchhiker, but was just walking. I didn't even think much about him as I passed him. I glanced back in my rearview mirror, and he was still trudging along. However, the farther I drove, the more I had this sense that I was supposed to turn around and give him a ride. "No, God," I said, "You can't really mean that," as I drove, trying to put my thoughts back on my shopping trip.

But the feeling persisted and became much stronger until

it almost felt as though it were suffocating me. It seemed as though the Holy Spirit was really making me uncomfortable. It persisted so that I could not dismiss it from my mind. The command to turn around became so strong that I gave in and finally prayed, "Alright, God, if this is from You, just protect me!"

I found a place to turn around and drove back toward the man. By this time he was more than two or three miles from me, but he quickly came into view once more, walking in my direction. I slowed down and had to pass him because he was on the other side of the street. As I did, he looked through the windshield and right into my eyes. I was scared, but when he looked into my eyes, I saw a kindness in them that was unexplainable. All at once, my spirit was filled with a wonderful kind of peace and I was no longer fearful. I knew then that this encounter was from God because I had a total peace like nothing I had ever experienced before.

As I made a U-turn to get on the same side of the road to stop, I had to look back to see if any cars were approaching. He was out of my sight for just a split second. This road was lightly traveled and no one else could be seen either way—just the road, the man, and my car. As I turned back toward the man, suddenly, in the blink of an eye, he had disappeared! No one else could have picked him up. There was no place for him to run to—no nearby homes, buildings, or even deep ditches. He had simply vanished!

I was dumbfounded. It affected me so much that I pulled off on the shoulder to gather my composure. Nothing in my life had prepared me for this kind of a happening. I just asked, "God why did this happen? What was the purpose in this? What for? Where did he go?"

With a deep peace still in my spirit, the thought struck me that this had been a test to see if I would be faithful, obedient, and willing to do something that would normally fill me with fear. I still don't really know the answer, but as I look back, I do believe it was a test.

The angel of the Lord encamps around those who fear him, and he delivers them (Psalm 34:7).

FOOD FOR THOUGHT: The Bible is full of angel stories; therefore, we have no other option than to talk of such beings. The teaching of the Scriptures is that these are created beings who have been chosen to minister in many different kinds of ways. If we are to be faithful students of the Word of God, we have no other choice than to appreciate everything God has made, including angels.

MISSIONARIES

Angel at My Side

Suddenly an angel of the Lord appeared and a light shone in the cell. He struck Peter on the side and woke him up. "Quick, get up!" he said, and the chains fell off Peter's wrists (Acts 12:7).

CHAPTER 70

ANGEL BODYGUARDS

The Christians in China during the internal uprising in 1927 were under all kinds of persecution. They were targets of looting, building burnings, executions, and more. Favorite targets of these vandals were mission compounds, hospitals, orphanages, and anything Christian.

A lady missionary is our source for this story.

"During a night of burning, looting, and shooting, when anarchists ran through the streets, our compound, which sheltered hundreds of women and girls who spent the time in prayer, went untouched."

But there's more to the story. The previous night, the missionary in charge of this particular mission, which was dedicated to sheltering homeless women and girls, had been laid low with a bad attack of malaria and a resulting high fever.

Some of the neighbors asked, "What are you planning to do when the looters attack your compound? What about all those promises of protection you have been preaching to us?

Who will you be trusting when the fires and robberies begin on your compound?"

Along with all the women and girls, this sick missionary spent much time in prayer. She pleaded, "Lord I have been teaching these people for many years to believe and trust in the promises of God. If You and Your promises fail in this time of disaster, I shall never again be able to open my mouth. Then I shall have to return home to America."

The next night when the anarchists came to the compound, she immediately was well enough to get up and walk among the frightened refugees in her care. She prayed with them and comforted them while disaster was taking place in the neighborhood all around them. But the mission compound and all who were inside were untouched.

The next morning, people from three different neighboring families asked, "Who were those four people—three were sitting and one was standing—who were quietly watching from the top of your house at the front of the compound?"

They answered, "No one was on our housetop."

The neighbors refused to believe the missionary. "We saw them with our own eyes. These men were awesome! When the looters came to the compound, they turned and ran because they became afraid. We saw it happen!"[1]

It was another teaching moment about the power of God that can send angelic guards for the protection of His children in times of distress.

"Because he [she] *loves me," says the Lord, "I will rescue him* [her]; *I will protect him* [her] *for he* [she] *acknowledges my name. He* [she] *will call upon me, and I will*

answer him [her]; *I will be with him* [her] *in trouble, I will deliver him* [her] *and honor him* [her]" (Psalm 91:14-15).

FOOD FOR THOUGHT: When facing impending disaster, where will you turn for help and deliverance? In today's world with terrorism on the rise, nuclear threats seem to be increasing. With the possibility of anarchy, inflation, the swine flu epidemic and more, where will you go for help? Our choices are three: do it yourself, rely on the government for help, or go to the Lord. God has promised He would be a "present help in times of need." He's my choice—how about you?

[1](Adapted from the *Pentecostal Evangel,* February 19, 1927. Used by permission.)

CHAPTER 71

SANDWICHED BETWEEN TWO ANGELS

*F*rankie is a missionary and speaker who has traveled extensively overseas as well as here in the States. She has counted at least twelve special angelic visitations. The following is one of them.

While speaking at a Hispanic church, I had an experience, much like some of those I had experienced in Africa.

The specific church in this story was about an hour from my home at the time. The roads were quite secluded for most of my solitary drive in the Ozarks of Missouri. On this particularly dark night, following a late service, I started to drive home. The highway was a blacktop with no center strip and no white guidelines on the side. A number of overgrown trees stood on either side, which made it like driving through a dark tunnel. No moon was shining because of the cloud cover, and it seemed that the inky darkness just sucked the light into it despite my use of bright headlights.

I began discussing this situation with the Lord and asked for His help. Almost immediately a black car came up behind, me, quickly passed, and settled in about two or three car lengths ahead. Checking my rear view mirror again, another black car approached and stayed behind me about two or three car lengths. I was sandwiched in for the rest of the drive home. An abundance of light guided me.

When I arrived in the city limits of my hometown, the lead car moved into the left lane of the four-lane highway to allow me to pass. I quickly glanced back, but no car was following me. I looked for the car in the left lane, and it too was suddenly gone. There were no exits, no turn ramp—only four lanes totally empty of cars except mine. God had come to my rescue one more time!

Another time while staying on the big island on the Hilo side of Hawaii, I was provided with an upstairs apartment. Returning home with the couple that had hosted me, I made my way up the steep set of stairs to the top landing. I turned to thank them for their assistance when I tripped and found myself falling with no handrail to grab hold of to catch myself and break the fall. As I fell, a hand or presence reached out and caught me on my chest and lifted me back to a standing position!

My host had seen what happened and agreed that only an angel on duty could have prevented a fall that might have been fatal. They said, "If we had not watched everything happen, we would not have believed it!" Again...angels to the rescue!

Still another time, my husband and I were returning home from a shopping trip. He was upset and driving too fast for conditions. We were speeding down a hill, and at the bottom was a large culvert. The neighborhood kids played there and rode bikes under the road through the culvert. We used this route often. As we topped the hill and started down, we were almost at the culvert when a little boy on his bike came onto the road right in front of us. We had no time to react and no place to turn to avoid him because of how fast we were going. I only had time to whisper, "Jesus!"

My husband slammed on the brakes, and the car skidded wildly. When we stopped, we were just about touching the fender of the boy's bike. My husband, who was by now shaking from the fright, said, "There is no way in the world I could have stopped in time to keep from running over the boy. Something stopped this car!"

The little boy was also shaking and crying. Immediately I jumped out and comforted him. Angels had been guarding all of us, in spite of the carelessness of the speeding driver.

"Don't be afraid," the prophet answered. "Those who are with us are more than those who are with them." And Elisha prayed, "O Lord, open his eyes so he may see." Then the Lord opened the servant's eyes, and he looked and saw the hills full of horses and chariots of fire all around Elisha (2 Kings 6:16-17).

FOOD FOR THOUGHT: Perhaps we should all pray the prayer of Elisha, "Open our eyes that we may see." We are so human and we can be so filled with fear when we have no reason to be afraid. You never know how many angels may be surrounding you at this very moment in your time of need.

THE TRAVEL AGENT ANGEL

*M*issionary-evangelist Melvin Jorgensen faced a tough situation when his plane arrived in Belgrade, Yugoslavia. He was scheduled to be the speaker at a conference the next morning at 8:30 in the town of Subotica, about 100 miles away, but the host pastor of that church was not there to meet Melvin as he had promised.

Furthermore, Jorgensen not only didn't know the language, but also he was not feeling well. How was he to find transportation to his destination? He had no currency that would have been negotiable in Yugoslavia to buy anything, let alone a bus ticket. What was he to do?

(What Melvin didn't know was that the pastor from Subotica had already come to the airport and inquired about the missionary's flight. He was told it had already arrived, and Jorgensen was not on it. So he had decided to return home in order to reach there before dark. He too was in a quandary wondering what to do about the conference beginning the next day.)

Back at the airport, Jorgensen decided he should at least

get on a shuttle that would take him to the bus terminal in the city. But he wondered, *What shall I do when I reach the terminal? How shall I find my way to Subotica? How shall I know which bus to take? How can I get some money with which to buy a bus ticket? How can I make myself understood?*

When the shuttle pulled into the terminal, Jorgensen's anxiety increased. A thousand people seemed to be milling about with dozens of buses coming and going. He was sick and lost.

Then a strange thing happened. As Melvin stepped off the shuttle, his attention was drawn to a man who stood there smiling at him. He was not even sure the smile was intended for him, but he smiled back.

The man was average height and appeared no different from the others, but he motioned for Jorgensen to follow him. Melvin did so because, after all, he had no other plan.

The terminal had many ticket windows, but which was the right one? He followed his guide until the man stopped at a window. The man talked to someone at the window, received a ticket, gave it to Jorgensen, and motioned for him to follow.

Outside was the bus-loading area. Again, which one should the missionary take? The man motioned for him to wait for his bus at an empty stall. He refused any payment and left.

The ordeal was not over. The ticket showed it was for the bus to Subotica but as time went on, no bus appeared where Jorgensen was standing. Ten, fifteen, twenty minutes passed. He began to wonder if this was the correct place to wait.

Then the special "travel agent" appeared once more, smiled, and indicated with motions he should continue to wait. Shortly afterwards, the bus pulled into the parking stall. Jorgensen boarded it, showed his ticket to the driver, and they were on their way to Subotica. He arrived safely, to the relief of the host pastor, and all went well at the conference.

Now an angel of the Lord said to Philip, "Go south to the road—the desert road—that goes down from Jerusalem to Gaza." So he started out, and on his way he met an Ethiopian eunuch, an important official in charge of all the treasury of Candace, queen of the Ethiopians (Acts 8:26-27).

FOOD FOR THOUGHT: Who was that travel agent character? Why was he seemingly waiting for a complete stranger? How could he have known this missionary-evangelist needed help for directions as well as money to buy the ticket? And how did he know the man's destination was Subotica? We may hesitate to speak dogmatically and claim this special travel-agent-helper was an angel, but tell me—do you have a better explanation?

CHAPTER 73

FOLLOWING ORDERS

*W*inifred Currie's favorite story comes from an experience in Belgium Congo, Zaire, when she was on an
evangelistic safari with Lucille Friesen, Martha Underwood,
and the nationals who were being trained in the Ndeya
School.

One morning while the three women were having their
private devotions, the Lord distinctly spoke to each of them
the same message: They were not to go to a cotton sale as
they had planned but were to specifically follow His guidance
as to where to stop beside the road and follow a path into a
village where God had a special person already prepared for
their coming.

Here's Winifred's story:

Our young guide disagreed with us about traveling to the
village. He said, "All the people will be working out in their
fields, and no one will be at home in the village."

But Mrs. Friesen replied, "You will witness a miracle of
grace today." So he reluctantly went along with us.

We followed the Lord's instruction exactly and when we came to the village, we met an elderly lady sitting by a small fire. She had scars like raised welts on her back, which we later learned were from beatings that she had received years earlier when she had been captured by an Azande raiding party. Apparently she had remained as a slave, unable to escape, and never saw her family again.

A boy was also in the village, and when he discovered our purpose, he began beating the drum to call the people out of their fields to hear our presentation. Soon everyone gathered and the message of the gospel of the cross of Jesus Christ in the Bangala language was given. This former slave woman's face began to light up as the name of *Yesu* (Jesus) was introduced as the name of the Son of God who had died for her sins. When we asked for those to make decisions to believe in Yesu, she began to speak excitedly in the Azande language.

She related that the night before, she was suddenly awakened from her sleep by a very bright light. Then she saw this person clothed in a white robe. She became afraid and cried out, "Who are you?" He spoke calmly and so kindly that her fear left her. He said, "Don't be afraid. Tomorrow I am sending My messengers to you, and they will tell you My name!" Then He disappeared.

She continued, "Now I know His name. It is Yesu and I want to believe in Him today!" The villagers were astonished and began to also respond to the gospel message that day.

We had the privilege of witnessing the greatest miracle among all the miracles we had seen in our ministry in the heart of Africa. That day, everyone in the village believed in Jesus as their Savior!

I, Jesus, have sent my angel to give you this testimony for the churches (Revelation 22:16).

FOOD FOR THOUGHT: There is no way to know how often angels have been involved in your life or mine. Maybe you will have one at your side the next time you go out. What a fantastic thought! But if they are seen or unseen, they are always on a mission that exalts our Lord and Savior Jesus Christ.

CHAPTER 74

THE MESSENGER

*Y*vonne (name changed) was seventeen, pregnant, penniless, alone, and very much afraid. She was at her wits' end, not knowing what to do. As she sat tearfully watching the sonogram of her baby, she saw the new life moving within her and knew at that moment an abortion would be out of the question. She cried herself to sleep every night. Then, one night an angel appeared to her in a dream. He said, "Don't be afraid. Everything will be fine because you and your baby will be well taken care of."

The angel pulled back the curtain of time and gave Yvonne a look into the future. She watched as her healthy, strong, and beautiful baby was placed by an angel into the arms of a wonderful, caring couple. The next scene showed the baby as a grown young lady, mature and happy. The angel also told her God was concerned about the baby and would work everything out for good for her unborn child. Then the angel turned to Yvonne and touched her with a light that seemed to give off a warm glow that stayed in her heart during the rest of her pregnancy.

When Yvonne awoke the next morning after the dream, she felt wonderful, loved, and at peace that everything would work out for the best. Later that day she was introduced to a lady who told her about a support group-home for unwed mothers, and Yvonne checked in the next day. There she found healing for her emotions and help about the choices she needed to make about her baby's future.

Her choice was to give birth and place the baby with a Christian adoption agency. While she held her baby for the last time in the hospital, Yvonne had her own dedication ceremony for her baby. She blessed the little girl with a long life and gave her to the Lord for protection, care, and keeping.

In Yvonne's story the angel appeared in a dream with a special message just for her. There is also a biblical story paralleling hers. About 2,000 years ago an angel appeared in a dream to a man named Joseph with instructions about another unborn child, and even gave him the child's name.

Later, Joseph had another dream in which an angel gave him the message to take the young child and his mother to Egypt to escape the plans of the wicked King Herod, who intended to kill the child Jesus.

The word "angel" as written in the original Greek and Hebrew language of the Bible means a "messenger" or "the messenger of God." There are all kinds of ways in which angels can get their message across to any of us in need of one.

But after he had considered this, an angel of the Lord appeared to him in a dream and said, "Joseph son of David, do not be afraid to take Mary home as your wife, because what is conceived in her is from the Holy Spirit. She will give birth to a son, and you are to give him the name of Jesus, because he will save his people from their sins." All this took place to fulfill what the Lord had said through the prophet (Matthew 1:20-22).

FOOD FOR THOUGHT: Hymn writer and author W.W. How wrote: "To comfort and to bless, to find a balm for woe, to tend the lonely and fatherless, is angels' work below." What a wonderful choice of words to describe the work of angels—to comfort, to bless and heal the broken-hearted, the lonely, and even the fatherless or motherless. Thank you, Lord, for knowing how and when to come to our aid.

CHAPTER 75

A HUGE ANGEL AT MY DOOR

*F*rankie Walker, a world traveler and lady minister of Springfield, Missouri shares with us an experience she had of angelic protection.

I had just returned from five months in Israel, Hong Kong, and Hawaii. I had been invited to housesit for some friends in Tulsa, Oklahoma, while they were gone. While there, the Holy Spirit told me that I would soon be moving there and directed my thinking to a specific apartment complex. Six months later, sure enough, this came to pass, and I signed a six-month lease on an apartment.

Shortly after I moved in, the lock on the door broke, and I asked the manager if he would be so kind as to fix it. He replied, "We only do repairs if you sign a one-year lease. Or if you continue to pay month to month, we will raise the rent $66 per month and do all the repairs you need."

Being a bit short of money and not knowing how long I would be in Tulsa, I felt strongly that I should not sign the yearly lease but simply trust God for provision and protection.

This apartment complex happened to be in a high crime area, and the door could be opened with just a slight push or even a gentle kick. I went to bed that night praying for protection because, naturally, I felt more than a bit uncomfortable knowing how vulnerable I was in the apartment. Falling asleep, I had a vision of a warrior angel standing outside my door, facing the door and turned in my direction. He was huge! He was taller than the top of the door—he was probably more than seven feet tall and very muscular. He stood with his arms crossed and feet spread apart in a very authoritative stance.

That night I slept like a baby, and I continued to do so every night for the next year and a half. My rent was never raised, and the lock was never fixed. When I left the apartment during the day or even for several days at a time as I traveled, I never worried about somebody breaking into it. I believe the angel was there both night and day. I lived there all that time with no incident!

Then I left for Hawaii. And that's another story. (In the next chapter we have one more angelic encounter from Frankie!)

Her word for us, which she wanted me to share with you is this: the Lord wants us to trust in Him and His protection at all times!

The heavens praise your wonders, O Lord, your faithfulness too, in the assembly of the holy ones. For who in the skies above can compare with the Lord? Who is like the Lord among the heavenly beings? In the council of the holy ones God is greatly feared; he is more awesome than all who surround him. O Lord God Almighty, who is like

*you? You are mighty, O Lord, and your faithfulness sur-
rounds you* (Psalm 89:5-8).

FOOD FOR THOUGHT: In all of these angelic encounters I have discovered they appear or are at work on our
behalf when there is a real need! What a comfort! But remember, we are asked to trust in God, not in the angels He
will send. And we are then to give praise to God and not to
angels when they have ministered to our needs.

CHAPTER 76

A BLACK ANGEL IN HAWAII

*F*rankie Walker continues with another of her encounters when she was in Hawaii:

While based in Oahu, a friend invited me to go with her to a street music festival in downtown Honolulu. We arrived to find a large crowd already in attendance. We were making our way from display booth to display booth, and the crowd was rapidly increasing. The crowd had grown so much that bodies were being pressed against each other. We began to panic and looked for a way out of the crowd, which stretched from sidewalk to sidewalk. Buildings solidly lined the street with no alleys or cross streets in sight. All the buildings were closed for the evening, so there was no place to go even if we could have moved there.

We could feel panic begin to grip the crowd. In the heat and the press, people began to faint and were carried along with the crowd because there was no place to lie down. More people were attempting to get into the festival from both ends, effectively blocking the crowd from getting out of the area. Now, I'm pretty strong for a lady and quite tall, but soon the weight of the crushing crowd unsteadied me several times. I nearly lost my footing, and to fall in this crowd would have been disastrous!

I began to pray that this crowd would not panic. I looked around and saw fear on many faces and felt that many people were on the verge of losing it. It was the worst mob scene I have ever witnessed. I continued to pray for help and a way out of the surging crowd.

All of a sudden I sensed I was no longer being pushed from behind or for that matter from either side or the front. I looked behind me and there was a tall, distinguished looking, clean cut, well-groomed black man, with peace and calmness all over his face. He stood head and shoulders above the crowd around us. He was completely relaxed and moved with a grace that was wonderful to watch. The jostling of the crowd didn't budge him one bit. He acted as our guard so no one brushed against us! He didn't say a word, simply nodded and smiled and stayed behind us for nearly an hour until we came to a clearing and could get away from the crowd. He never moved from being our guardian all this time.

As we managed to get clear of the crowd, I turned to thank him and he was gone! Not more than a few seconds before I had looked at him. We searched everywhere, but he was nowhere to be found. He had just disappeared, but not into the crowd or we could have spotted him, for he was so tall. Then I knew that he had been an angel sent to protect us.

A policeman was standing nearby and I asked him about the situation, and he said it was a miracle no one had panicked to the point of screaming, or many could have been trampled. I asked him if he had seen our "guide" and he said, "Only you two ladies."

If you make the Most High your dwelling—even the Lord, who is my refuge—then no harm will befall you, no disaster will come near your tent. (Psalm 91:9-10).

FOOD FOR THOUGHT: Perhaps you're thinking, *How is it possible that Frankie can have more than one encounter with angels, and I haven't even had one?* Perhaps they have been at work in your life a number of times, and you didn't recognize their presence. In Frankie's two encounters, one appeared in a dream, and one appeared in the flesh. The Bible explains that many of us have entertained angels and not been aware of it. "Do not forget to entertain strangers, for by so doing some people have entertained angels without knowing it" (Hebrews 13:2).

CHAPTER 77

ANGELS ON GUARD

This happened in East Africa during the Mau Mau uprisings, which took place in 1956, and was told to me by Phil Plotts, son of missionary Morris Plotts. Here's the story:

A band of roving Mau Maus came upon the village of Lauri, surrounded it, and killed every inhabitant, including women and children, approximately 300 in all. Not more than three miles away was the Rift Valley School, a private school where missionary children were being educated. Immediately upon leaving the carnage of Lauri, the Mau Maus came with spears, bows and arrows, clubs, and torches toward the school with the same intentions of complete destruction.

Of course, you can imagine the fear of those little inhabitants and their instructors housed in the boarding school. Word had already reached them about the devastation wreaked upon Lauri. There was no place to flee with the little children and women, and their only resource was to pray.

Soon, out of the darkness of the night, lighted torches appeared, and quickly a ring of these terrorists circled the school. Shouts and curses could be heard from the Mau Maus as they began to advance. All of a sudden, when they were close enough to throw spears, they stopped and inexplicably began to run the other way!

A call had gone out to the authorities and an army had been sent, but they arrived after the Mau Maus had already left. The army spread out and searched for the rebels until they captured the entire band, including their leaders.

They later appeared before the judge at their trial. The leader was the first one called to the witness stand. The judge questioned: "On this particular night, did you kill the inhabitants of Lauri?"

"Yes."

"Was it your intent to do the same killing at the missionary school in Rift Valley?"

"Yes."

"Well, then," asked the judge, "why did you not complete your mission? Why didn't you attack the school?"

(Allow me to break in upon the story with a note: This Mau Mau leader was a heathen, a person who had never read the Bible and never been exposed to Christianity, or told about angels.)

The leader replied to the judge, "We were on our way to attack and destroy all the people and the school, but as we came closer, all of a sudden, between us and the school, there were huge men dressed in white and each had a flaming sword. We became afraid and ran to hide."

Later, when the children and instructors were asked if they saw these same men, they all replied with a resounding no. The missionary in charge of the school hadn't seen any angels, only the flight of the frightened Mau Mau band. An ancient proverb says, "When angels come, the devils leave."

For he will command his angels concerning you to guard you in all your ways; they will lift you up in their hands, so that you will not strike your foot against a stone (Psalm 91:11-12).

FOOD FOR THOUGHT: None of us can fathom how often angels may have been involved in our lives. While angels can become visible, our eyes don't ordinarily see them. It's like not being able to see the dimensions of a nuclear field or the structure of atoms or electricity flowing through a copper wire. Our ability to sense reality is very limited, but that doesn't change the fact that angels have been present!

CHAPTER 78

THE LITTLE OLD LADY ANGEL

A wonderful missionary friend of ours (name with-held) was on a special assignment to Israel in 1990. It was during the period of time when Saddam Hussein was firing Scud missiles into Jerusalem as well as other parts of Israel and threatening to send many more. Naturally, people were on edge. This missionary tells her story:

A friend and I were walking through the Arab quarters in Jerusalem when one of those missiles landed near enough for us to hear the explosion. A moment later we heard another noise coming from behind us. Before I could jump out of the way, an Arab merchant with a large metal cart loaded with heavy boxes came barreling down the slightly sloped street and hit me directly in the back, just below the shoulder blades. The hit was hard because he had been running with his cart down the street. I was stunned, badly hurt, and knocked to the ground. I quickly went into shock.

Another Arab merchant helped me to sit up and assisted

me to a low stool. This kind man immediately began to apologize for the recklessness of his fellow merchant. I sat for some moments attempting to gather my senses and assess the pain. I realized that I had broken ribs and other injuries.

Finally, I managed to stand to my feet with the confession, "Lord, by your stripes I am healed."

Another shopkeeper among the gathering crowd asked, "Lady, how did you manage to get back up? How are you able to stand on your feet?"

I was aware of people surrounding me. I had barely managed to remain standing because of the pain in my back. I suspected I also had an injury to my spine because the pain was excruciating.

All of a sudden, a little old lady, looking to be about seventyish stepped up to me, took both of my hands in hers, looked me in the eyes with the most compassionate look I'd ever seen and said only one word: "Peace!" Instantly my strength returned, my knees quit trembling, the effects of the shock were gone, and all the pain completely disappeared! I had received an instant healing!

I turned my head to thank the kind merchant for his help while still holding the little old lady's hands, and then turned back to thank her, but she had vanished! The crowd was small and I could see up and down the street, but she was gone. She had just disappeared while she was holding my hands!

I don't know about you, but this is just another confirmation of the reality of angels. This is an interesting appearance. I've never had anyone describe an angel as a "little old lady about seventyish." Well, why not?

But for you who revere my name, the sun of righteousness will rise with healing in its wings. And you will go out and leap like calves released from the stall (Malachi 4:2).

FOOD FOR THOUGHT: Do you have any friends who have criticized you for believing in angels? Don't let them bother you. You're in good company! Remember that in the Bible, the existence of angels is assumed. And did you know there are more than 300 direct references to them? J.M. Wilson wrote, "There is nothing unnatural or contrary to reason about belief in angels."

CHAPTER 79

TWO AFRICAN ANGELS

The place is the Sudan, in Northeast Africa; the city is Khartoum; the time is 1989 during the winter season. It's the country where an indigenous missionary family was born—father, mother, and four children. Let's hear their story as this Sudanese lady, now living as a naturalized citizen in the US tells it:

Our home had been used as a place of rest and refuge for a number of missionaries, in particular the Sudan Interior Mission. The situation was critical because of the ruling Muslim government which demanded our presence in the mission to divert attention from the foreign missionaries.

It so happens the mention of angels is a popular topic among us. Everybody—both Muslims and Christians—believed in angels. It was a subject that could likely be discussed almost every day.

It was also at this critical time that the door had opened for us to migrate to the US. Much was happening—events were swirling about us over which we didn't seem to have much control, and it was nearing the time when three of our children were to leave. Suddenly the government decided to take away from us our adopted four-year-old son, Samir, and place him in a Muslim family for their adoption. In so doing he was to be raised as a Muslim, not a Christian.

On top of this, one of our children was sick and confined to a bedroom on the ground floor. I had worries upon worries. Panic and fear began to grip my heart.

One evening this cup of suffering and weariness just overflowed. I went into my closet in our bedroom to pray. I prayed until I fell asleep.

I was awakened suddenly and saw a light coming in from the doors to the closed balcony. Two figures stood against the drawn curtains. My heart was beating with the thought that this was a night robbery. I sat up and covered my face with my hands and then slowly opened them.

The two figures came nearer. They were tall, and their heads were wrapped in traditional African floral turbans matching their long elaborate robes. They spoke in a quiet tone in our native language.

One of them said, "Do not be afraid."

The other said, "We are sent to encourage you. God wants you to know this: YOU ARE NOT ALONE!"

I was trembling and asked, "Are you angels? If you are, then come and stand behind the big chair."

To my shock and amazement, they glided and danced their way to the chair. They were beautiful and silhouetted against the light they brought with them. Then and there I sensed a great peace of God. I asked, "Why are you dressed so?"

The second angel replied, "This is how we were sent

here," obviously meaning to Africa where floral designs are very traditional.

The other angel spoke, "You are loved, both you and your family. We encourage your faith because you encourage the helpless and insecure."

Then they disappeared, gradually out of my sight as silently as they had entered. I was alone once more, but I was completely refreshed in body and in spirit. I was thankful that now I could face the remainder of what was before us.

On the twenty-fourth day of the first month, as I was standing on the bank of the great river, the Tigris, I looked up and there before me was a man dressed in linen, with a belt of the finest gold around his waist. He body was like chrysolite, his face like lightning, his eyes like flaming torches, his arms and legs like the gleam of burnished bronze, and his voice like the sound of a multitude. I, Daniel, was the only one who saw the vision; the men with me did not see it, but such terror overwhelmed them that they fled and hid themselves (Daniel 10:4-7).

FOOD FOR THOUGHT: Daniel was the only one who saw the angel, but others felt the effect of that presence. Most angel stories have to do with a single person who may have been the only one to experience the appearance. Once again, we must trust the messenger as to what they have seen or experienced since we have attempted to weed out any stories that didn't pass the biblical test.

CHAPTER 80

WHAT BIG GUY?

This happened on an Indian Reservation in the state of North Dakota. (Names have been changed.) Marvin Ellsworth is the pastor of an Indian mission church on the reservation.

The day started out like any other day on the North Dakota prairie—a bit on the windy side, but a clear and bright, sunny summer day. Suddenly an Indian boy about fifteen or sixteen years old came running down the road toward the mission. Pastor Ellsworth looked out the window and went out the door to meet the boy. He was out of breath but managed to get out the news that a fight had broken out between two factions.

The pastor asked, "Did you call the sheriff?"

He replied, "Yes, but he is out on another call and can't come."

Again the pastor asked, "Have you asked anybody else for help?"

"No."

"Well, how many are involved?"

"About thirty to thirty-five people."

Since no one else was available to quiet things down, the pastor said, "Come with me," as he quickly ran to the van. When the two of them drove up to where the men were fighting, he quickly sized up the situation. They were all armed with baseball bats, knives, clubs, lead pipes and guns. The situation was not good, and fear gripped the pastor. He quickly prayed a fervent prayer for protection and stepped out of the van. The fighting immediately stopped, and all combatants turned their attention toward the pastor.

He says, "I spoke for about twenty minutes. I thought it was probably the best sermon I have ever preached. I said things but wasn't sure where they came from. I quoted scripture I didn't even know. And they all stood completely focused on me, still holding their weapons. They didn't pay any attention to each other or who their enemy was. The longer I spoke, the bolder I felt. When I finished speaking, quietly each of the combatants made their way to their cars or pickups and drove off. There was no more fighting or even taunts. And you can only guess at how relieved I felt.

"I noticed that the two leaders started talking to each other and motioned at me. I began to feel fear gripping my heart. These guys were big—much larger than I am. They slowly began walking toward me. I didn't know whether to run or jump in my van and attempt a quick get-a-way or what. I just froze in apprehension as they came closer. Both were armed, and neither smiled or in any way showed any emotion. But they kept on slowly moving in my direction.

"They stopped about three feet in front of me. I was cornered with my back against my van and the two of them on each side of me. I looked from one to the other. Then one of the leaders spoke, 'Tell us who the great big guy is who stood behind you while you were speaking and who is now standing over there.'

"Pastor Ellsworth and I whirled around to look but couldn't see any big guy, but these two faction leaders clearly saw him. Then it dawned on me—God had sent a guardian angel!"

This particular incident marked the beginning of many good things at the church mission. Barriers were broken and many of the Native Americans began attending the church with the pastor who had the "big guy" for protection!

> *"Don't be afraid," the prophet answered. "Those who are with us are more than those who are with them." And Elisha prayed, "O Lord, open his eyes so he may see." Then the Lord opened the servant's eyes, and he looked and saw the hills full of horses and chariots of fire all around Elisha* (2 Kings 6:16-17).

FOOD FOR THOUGHT: Angelic protection is a constant theme running through many angel stories. We have been taught about guardian angels and that each of us, especially children, have one. One premise for the guardian angel is based on the statement of Jesus in Matthew 18:10, "See that you do not look down on one of these little ones. For I tell you that their angels in heaven always see the face of my Father in heaven." What a comforting concept—a special guardian on duty 24/7 for us!

HEALING AND SALVATION

Angels to the Rescue

Are not all angels ministering spirits sent to serve those who will inherit salvation? (Hebrews 1:14)

CHAPTER 81

AN ANGEL TO THE RESCUE

*M*y mother, Ruth, is ninety-eight years young, lives in her own home, and still drives her car to the grocery store. Life has been good and productive for her. She has been a director of senior ministries for many years and still is active in leading the seniors in her home church. She's an immaculate dresser and an accomplished seamstress as well as being a great cook. She still bakes and cooks a number of special Norwegian dishes for the people she entertains. She has a pacemaker, but other than that, her doctor says nothing is wrong with Ruth. She has an active life.

Perhaps one secret of long life is living in north central Minnesota. Two winters ago, I called and asked, "Mom, how cold is it today?"

She replied, "Twenty below zero."

"So what are you doing?" I asked her.

"I've been outside shoveling snow," she replied.

"Mom, you have renters in the basement who are supposed to shovel your snow."

"Well, they don't shovel it right." (Now how can you not shovel snow correctly?)

That's not all. Her older sister, Evangeline, is 104 years old. She lives on the family farm by herself, but her family has made provisions for a home visit from a nurse every day. "Vangie," as she is known to everyone, offers freshly baked cookies to all who visit and plays the piano for them even though she happens to be stone deaf (an affliction that struck her in her mid-forties).

What a great attitude she has. She tells one and all, "The Lord isn't finished with me yet." In three more years her younger son will celebrate a fiftieth wedding anniversary, and Vangie said, "I'll be there for that!" Of course, Vangie is the oldest resident in her county. I have digressed, but I thought you might enjoy a bit of background for our story.

Last summer while my mother was tending to her flowers in her small concrete patio off the kitchen, she tripped over her very large and spoiled cat, Mitzi, and fell backwards into the adjoining rock garden. She fell flat, hitting her head on the rocks and was knocked unconscious. When she regained her senses, she knew immediately that her situation was not good. Her head was in pain as well as her back, ribs, and one hip. In her words, "The pain was awful, and I couldn't get up!" She was positive some bones were broken. The neighbors are quite a distance away and could not hear her cry for help. She lay on her back and simply prayed, "Jesus, help me."

She told me, "It happened in an instant. All of a sudden, I was on my feet and standing in my kitchen next to the table. All the pain was gone! A man was standing right next to me. His eyes were the most remarkable ones I had ever seen. I asked him, 'Who are you? How did you get here?' He looked at me without a word and slowly faded away. Without being told, in my spirit I instantly knew it was an angel who had been sent to help me."

> *But you have come to Mount Zion, to the heavenly Jerusalem, the city of the living God. You have come to thousands upon thousands of angels in joyful assembly* (Hebrews 12:22).

FOOD FOR THOUGHT: As a son with an aged mother, I am comforted to know she has had a ministering angel meet her needs. The distance between us is too great for me to be on call at all times. Her experience gives credence to the concept that we all have at least one guardian angel. We are privileged to have a God who not only knows when a common sparrow falls but also when one of His elderly saints takes a tumble. What an awesome God we serve!

CHAPTER 82

DOES ANYONE CARE?

*A*rthur Berg wrote, "I was not dreaming. I did not have a vision. I was wide awake that day when suddenly the room was filled with the sounds of singing and music blending in beautiful harmony." Where was it coming from? How? Why?

This story is fascinating. Arthur and Anna Berg were alone in a mission station at Masis-Rutchuru in the Kivu District of the Congo. For days, Anna and her daughter, Agnes, had been sick with malaria. Anna's temperature rose to 105.2 degrees. She became weaker, her voice was only a faint whisper, and she was drifting in and out of a semi-coma.

Her condition was so critical that Arthur called a group of Congolese Christians to join him in prayer for Anna. They were more than willing.

Just a bit later, in frustration, Arthur stepped out of their humble thatched roof home into the African night. The clear tropical black sky was filled with myriads of stars that seemed so near. He looked toward the northwest and their home in the United States, ten thousand miles away and prayed, "O God, does anyone at home know of our predicament? Does anyone care?"

Years later, after returning to America, he received his answer. A lady in Minneapolis who was a friend of the family asked him, "Were you and Anna in any trouble at this time in the Congo? I saw your face one time and was seized with a burden. I went to God in prayer and prayed until I had a peace about your need." They compared notes and learned it was the exact time when Arthur had prayed in the night.

But on that desperate African night, Arthur knew nothing about this woman praying. He returned inside, opened a hymn book at their little folding pump organ, and began to sing these words:

> He soothes me in sorrow with songs in the night,
> And inspires me with hope anew;
> He fills me with courage my battles to fight,
> Was there ever a friend so true?

The song's title is "Was There Ever a Friend So True?" As Arthur sang, suddenly the room was filled with indescribable music. He was no longer alone! Singing with him was a choir like none that he had ever heard before or since. A strong presence was in the room. He looked around him, and the Congolese Christians were still praying while the angels were singing in English about Jesus Christ, a Friend who was near.

It was quite a moment that was suddenly interrupted by a Congolese who shouted, "Madame, *anakufa!* Madame, *anakufa!*" (Madame is dying! Madam is dying!) Quickly Arthur ran to her bedside, not to witness her dying, but to see her hands raised in worship. The fever had broken! Her temperature had fallen.

Arthur then checked the bed where his daughter, Agnes, was lying. She too was healed! The next day both mother and daughter were able to resume normal life activities. Later Anna said that in the middle of her suffering, what seemed like a ball of fire had touched her head and gone throughout her entire body.

These events had all taken place simultaneously. When Arthur was out in the yard praying, when the African Christians were praying, and when the little lady in Minnesota was praying, the answer came. A choir of angels was sent to help a weary missionary and to restore a wife and daughter back to health. What an amazing God!

For he will command his angels concerning you to guard you in all your ways; they will lift you up in their hands (Psalm 91:11-12).

FOOD FOR THOUGHT: What a wonderful, thoughtful, loving God we serve—a Friend who understands our needs in time of distress and ministers to us accordingly.

CHAPTER 83

THE RESCUING ANGEL

A lady from the state of Montana had traced me down and phoned to share her story. This was one, she said, that no one else knew about other than her parents, not even her husband. She decided to give me permission to use it in case it might encourage someone else.

This woman was eight years old when the story happened. She and three other neighbor kids were playing together in the street in front of their homes. One thing led to another and pretty soon they were participating in an activity which had been forbidden. Forbidden fruit that has some risk attached seems to increase the excitement. Parked in the street was a 1940 Ford coupe with a long sloping trunk, and they began climbing up on the top and sliding down the trunk. It was her turn once again and down she came, dead center on the trunk and impaled herself on the middle bumper guard, which pierced through and into her vagina and rectum. Immediately she screamed in pain and the blood flowed freely. The other neighbor kids became really scared and ran away leaving her alone and unable to free herself.

"Almost immediately," she told me, "a man dressed in a beautiful gray suit, white shirt, and tie came running up to the car. He reached down and lovingly, carefully lifted me off the bumper guard. He talked to me in a comforting tone of voice, telling me that I would be all right. The pain, which had been unbearable, quickly stopped as he carried me to our front door. He knocked on the door and my mother answered. She was understandably upset with the sight of so much blood on my dress, legs, socks, and shoes. The man gently said, 'You should take her to your doctor to be examined.' Then he handed me over to my mother's arms and left.

"My mother quickly carried me out to our car, hopped in the front seat, and backed down the driveway and into the street for the short trip to the emergency room. But before she shifted gears to proceed, she stopped and got out, thinking she should express her thanks to the kind man, but he was nowhere to be found. At the hospital they carefully examined me and could find nothing wrong, nor was there any part of my body hurt. Yes, they saw all the blood. I explained what had happened, and they just shook their heads. They sent me home with a very grateful mother.

"Years passed, but my mother was always concerned about any internal injuries I may have sustained. But everything seemed to function normally for a growing girl. After I was married, she was concerned whether or not I could have children, but that was happily settled too. Today I am the mother of three healthy kids and a happily married woman with no female problems of any kind!

"I've often thought about that kind man in the gray suit. The only conclusion I have come to is that it was an angel on assignment. Following that hospital visit, my mother had inquired if anyone had seen such a man in our small town where everybody knew about everybody else and their business, but found no one who had." Before hanging up the phone, she thanked me for listening to her story so that someone else might be encouraged.

Praise the Lord, you his angels, you mighty ones who do his bidding, who obey his word. Praise the Lord, all his heavenly hosts, you his servants who do his will (Psalm 103:20-21).

FOOD FOR THOUGHT: We must remember that the object of our faith is the most important, and that object is to be God. Would you trust and love Him more if you were to see an angel today? We are to love Him even if we have never seen an angel or experienced an angelic visit or deliverance. God desires us to love Him for who He is, not because He has angels at His command.

CHAPTER 84

FLYING ON HER OWN

The next story is from Bonnie, who learned a valuable lesson through her angelic encounter.

My experience happened one afternoon in December. My husband, Bob, had been cutting down a tree in the front yard. He was finished and came in to take a shower. I went out to inspect his job and saw the front yard was a mess with brush and limbs everywhere. I decided to clean it up and piled up about a third of it when I began feeling pressure in my chest. Immediately I knew something was terribly wrong. I barely made it back inside the house.

Bob knew he quickly needed to get me help and called Dr. Mack to tell him what was happening and ask what might be wrong. Dr. Mack said immediately, "It's her heart" and called an ambulance to take me to the hospital. Naturally, I was praying all the time.

I was loaded onto a gurney and soon lost consciousness. When I woke up, the doctors told me I had had a heart attack, and they had cleared out two clogged arteries. They said

I needed a triple bypass surgery, which I didn't want but agreed to have. Before I could have the surgery, I had a second heart attack. They loaded me onto another gurney and rushed me to the emergency unit because I had passed out.

The next thing I heard was a doctor calling, "Bonnie...Bonnie...." I managed to open my eyes. That was two heart attacks in three days! The doctors decided they could not do the bypass surgery because of my fragile condition. They also told us they weren't sure how long I would survive.

My pastor told my husband, "Bob, we are going to believe God for a miracle." A friend of ours visited and said, "Bonnie, I believe God has given me a promise for you. Read in Psalm 118:17, 'I will not die but live, and will proclaim what the Lord has done!" I had other encouraging visitors as well.

On the sixth day, as I lay in the intensive ward, I began hearing the most beautiful heavenly music. I was wide awake and Bob was with me. I asked him, "Do you hear that music?" When he said he didn't hear it, I realized it was only for me.

Bob said, "Well, tell me some of the words you're hearing."

I was able to tell him some words as the music continued. Later we determined the words were from an old song, "Life's Railway to Heaven," which had been composed in 1917. I couldn't recall all the words, but just enough to get the drift of what it was saying.

Following the music, angels began appearing, one at a time. They were light golden and sort of fluffy in appearance. They came out of the wall of my room. I counted them one at a time, and a total of seven surrounded my bed. They didn't say anything but just stood there for a while and then disappeared through the wall.

I told Bob, "I don't know what the Lord is doing, but I felt the greatest presence of love and peace." Bob was so happy for me, but he was disappointed that he hadn't seen anything.

I spent ten days in the intensive care unit. On my tenth day there, the doctor took the heart pump off and told Bob, "We've done all we can do. She might not make it. She is going to have to fly on her own." Bob called the church for someone to come and be with him if I was about to die.

Then I was moved to a regular room, and the next day I was discharged. I was well enough to fly on my own! As I write this, five years have passed and I am doing just great and have no more heart problems!

The chariots of God are tens of thousands and thousands of thousands angels (Psalm 68:17).

FOOD FOR THOUGHT: Have you ever wondered how many angels exist? The above verse gives us a bit of a clue. Jesus said he could have called legions of angels to help so it seems to me there are more than enough are available to go around to be of help to all of us when needed.

CHAPTER 85

A SUDDEN DEATH
SYNDROME

*D*ick Forkner of Salem, Oregon, experienced the following story, something he will never forget:

My pastor was in the middle of his Sunday morning sermon when I felt warm and removed my jacket. It seemed as though my lungs weren't getting enough oxygen. Then a yellow sheet seemed to be pulled down in front of my eyes. The next thing I remember I was looking up into the face of a paramedic.

My wife, Evelyn, said she had touched my hand, and it was cold and damp. My head fell onto her shoulder, and I stopped breathing. She yelled for someone to call 911.

Four men laid me in the aisle and an off-duty para-medic and a nurse rushed to my side. The wife of our senior adult minister told Evelyn, "We have to wait for the ambulance, but God doesn't have to wait." Those words calmed my wife, who had seen her first husband die in her arms.

Suddenly another figure came up the aisle, not running or

walking. He just seemed to appear. He said to Evelyn, "I'm a doctor." He knelt beside me, shook his head no, and then hit me quite forcibly in the chest. At that same moment, my pastor and the entire congregation started to pray, and I began to breathe.

The ambulance took me to the hospital. Later I attempted to contact those who had assisted me. When I asked about the "doctor," everyone gave the same reply, "There was no doctor." My wife and a retired minister were the only ones who had seen him. They both gave an identical account, but nobody else had seen this man.

The medical staff said I should have had heart and lung damage, but I had none. They also said the only way my heart could have been quickly started was by a hard blow to the chest. No one, except my wife and the retired minister, had seen the "doctor" give the blow to my chest. However, I did have a sore spot there the next day.

During nearly a month of testing, no reason could be found for either my sudden collapse or remarkable recovery. It was medically determined I had had "sudden death syndrome."

I know it was a messenger of God who brought me back...and it was the Lord who healed me.

My strength is gone and I can hardly breathe. Again the one who looked like a man touched me and gave me strength. "Do not be afraid, O man highly esteemed," he said. "Peace! Be strong now; be strong!" (Daniel 10:17-19)

FOOD FOR THOUGHT: Angels seem to be able to assume just about any kind of form from bright and shining beings of light to a very human form. In this situation, one appeared like a doctor and acted like a doctor. But isn't it strange that only two people saw this "doctor" in action? Here is another example of an angel at work, carrying out a single mission of mercy with exquisite timing!

CHAPTER 86

DO ANGELS KNOW CPR?

*O*n a cold early December night in 1990 Douglas Craig, newly trained and graduated from the police academy, was on duty. He had been assigned to work a patrol at the Denver Airport. Making his rounds, he started down a long, deserted walkway. Quite a ways ahead of him, he watched as an older man stopped, collapsed, and slumped to the floor against the wall.

Doug ran quickly to help the man. He was doing his best to try to remember his training as he reached to check a pulse and found none. The man had also stopped breathing.

This was Doug's first emergency, and he was alone with no backup. He immediately called for medical help on his police radio. The sterile classroom training he had recently taken seemed so long ago. He sensed that if he didn't do something quickly, the man would die before help arrived. What could he do? He breathed a prayer, "Jesus, please help me. Help me to know what to do."

Just then, coming from behind him, he heard a woman's voice saying, "I'm an emergency room nurse. I'll do the chest compression if you will do the CPR breathing."

Doug wondered where she came from. He hadn't heard any steps behind him or seen anyone coming down the walkway. The floor was hard surfaced, so any steps would have been heard from a long way off, echoing off the hard surfaces of the walls and ceilings as well. Shrugging off his questions, he focused at the task at hand.

Doug began the mouth-to-mouth resuscitation while the nurse did the chest compressions. When the paramedics arrived and took over, the man began to revive.

"Then," Doug says, "the most peculiar thing happened. I stood up and looked around for the nurse so I could thank her, but she was gone! No one was there! The walkway was long, and no exits were handy. She should have been easily seen. She had appeared out of nowhere when I desperately needed help; when the crisis was over, she had simply vanished!"

Do you think angels know how to perform CPR? Would an angel have to resort to CPR to revive someone?

To this day, Douglas Craig believes angels know CPR, well at least one who took the form of a woman and appeared out of nowhere when she was needed in Denver.

As a policeman to this day, Doug is one cop who always makes his patrols with a sense that there can be divine help in times of real need.

And my God will meet all your needs according to His glorious riches in Christ Jesus (Philippians 4:19).

FOOD FOR THOUGHT: Here's something to think about—angels never die! Therefore, the angels we will meet in heaven will be the same ones we have read about in the Bible. Think of the excitement in meeting Gabriel and Michael and the one who shut the mouths of the lions in the den for Daniel. What about the one who rolled away the stone from the tomb of Jesus? Then we will want to meet the angel who led Peter out of jail and many more. Angels will always be only angels for all of eternity. And God will always be God throughout eternity!

CHAPTER 87

ANGELS COMING FOR TO TAKE ME HOME

*T*he above words are taken from a wonderful, old spiritual. But there may be more truth than wishful thinking in them as regards to the homegoing of some of God's wonderful people. Let's take a quick look at some bedside or even deathbed experiences.

When D.L. Moody, the evangelist, was aware death was nearing, he said, "Earth recedes, heaven opens before me." To those who had gathered at his bedside, it seemed as if he were dreaming, but he said, "No, this is no dream. It is beautiful; it is like a trance. If this is death, it is sweet. There is no valley here. God is calling me, and I must go."

After having been given up for dead, Moody revived long enough to indicate that God permitted him to see beyond this life. He said he had been "within the gates and beyond the portals and caught a glimpse of familiar faces whom he had loved and in the presence of a great heavenly host."

Phillips Brooks, the composer of "O Little Town of Bethlehem," was a great preacher/orator of the nineteenth century. When he died, a little girl of five told her mother, "Mother, how happy the angels will be!"

Billy Graham wrote, "When my maternal grandmother died, the room seemed to fill with a heavenly light. She sat up in bed and almost laughingly said, 'I see Jesus. He has His arms outstretched toward me. I see Ben (her husband who had died some years earlier) and I see angels.' She slumped over, absent from the body but present with the Lord."

Lucille O'Neil, had a beautiful experience at death. She had been in a tubercular hospital for some years. The night before her death she talked about the sweet-smelling fragrance of the beautiful flowers and the angel who stood at the pathway leading through the flower garden. Occasionally, the angel waved to her. "It was as if they were in the room with me," she said. Later she pointed to the ceiling and said, "There the angel is now, waving again. He is standing among the most beautiful roses I have ever seen. Can you smell the roses?"

Sibil Spruill from Houston was taken to Herman Hospital for treatment following a severe asthma attack. She explained her near-death experience as "something so beautiful and pleasant that there are not sufficient descriptive terms in man's language to aptly relate the reality of heaven." She saw white robes on manlike forms but saw no faces. After being ushered into an atmosphere of brightness and beauty, she eventually came to a resting place that seemed to be a waiting area before entering heaven. The white robed angels stood on either side of her as she looked upon the breathtaking beauty of the heavenly scene before her.

The angels on either side of her seemed to be discussing whether to take her into the beautiful brightness that stretched before her or to return her to earth. The same robed angelic forms then lifted her from the place where she was standing and moved swiftly toward earth. An instant later she found her spirit entering her body again, in the same way it had departed, almost as if a vacuum had pulled it into the body.

When she awoke, the asthma attack was gone! And later, she discovered she had been completely healed of asthma and lived for many more years!

Therefore, we are always confident and know that as long as we are at home in the body we are away from the Lord. We live by faith, not by sight. We are confident, I say, and would prefer to be away from the body and at home with the Lord. So we make it our goal to please him, whether we are at home in the body or away from it. For we must all appear before the judgment seat of Christ, that each one may receive what is due him for the things done while in the body, whether good or bad (2 Corinthians 5:6-10).

FOOD FOR THOUGHT: I believe that death can be a beautiful experience! With that belief we can look forward to it and welcome it with anticipation. The Bible plainly states, "Precious in the sight of the Lord is the death of His saints!" (Psalm 116:15) David said it so well for all of us, "Even though I walk through the valley of the shadow of death, I will fear no evil, for You are with me" (Psalm 23:4). Are you ready for life or death? No one is really ready to die who has not placed confidence in the sacrifice of Jesus Christ for their sins. Death is our greatest crisis. And we have the assurance that He will have His angels ready to gather us in their arms and carry us gloriously into our heavenly reward! Anticipate it! It's awesome to contemplate!

CHAPTER 88

SARAH'S ANGEL

$\mathcal{S}$arah (name changed) recently had a nightmarish experience and lived to tell the story. She was returning to her car, which was parked in the mall parking lot when she was accosted by two men, who at gunpoint forced her into their car. They blindfolded her, tied her up, and hurriedly drove out to a deserted stretch of woods where they raped her. Before her attackers left, one of them pulled out a pistol and shot her three times, and then they both fled.

Several hours passed, she had no recollection of how many, but somehow she started to revive. She managed to struggle to her feet. She futilely searched for her shoes but couldn't find them. In her bare feet she stumbled, fell, crawled, and walked out to the country road. She knew if she was to have some help, she'd have to walk the miles to town. With her goal in focus, she began to make her way on the harsh, sharp gravel of the roadway, stopping frequently to rest. She would walk and fall, then sit for a while to gather strength and get up to go again. She began to fear she would die before she found help.

She prayed and asked God to please send someone to help her. In her weakened state and nearly delirious with pain and the loss of blood, she suddenly felt like she was being helped along. It was almost like being carried, and she didn't stumble or fall any more. Quickly she reached the first home on the edge of town, and at that moment, it seemed to her as if she were placed gently back on the ground.

A light was on in the house. She managed to walk up the three steps onto the porch and knocked on the door. A young woman answered, took one long look at Sarah, and crumpled to the floor in a dead faint. Her husband stepped over his wife to help Sarah inside to a couch on which to lie down.

He quickly phoned 911 for an ambulance, then went back to help his wife, who was beginning to revive. When she felt better and was seated in an easy chair across from the couch, Sarah managed a weak, wan smile and whispered, "I'm sorry that I frightened you like this. I know I must look terrible."

The wife replied, "No, that's not why I fainted. I saw this great big shining angel holding you up as you stood in the doorway!"

Later at the emergency room of the hospital where the ER doctor examined her, he noted that even though she had covered several miles on the rough gravel road, she didn't have even a scratch or bruise on her bare feet! Furthermore he couldn't understand how the three gunshot wounds had closed up so she didn't bleed to death. She also seemed to have no internal bleeding or injury to her organs. In fact, after a night's rest and stitches to close the wounds, Sarah was able to walk out of the hospital under her own power and return to her normal life. She had completely recovered from her ordeal!

The Egyptians mistreated us and our fathers, but when we cried out to the Lord, He heard our cry and sent an angel and brought us out of Egypt (Numbers 20:15-16).

FOOD FOR THOUGHT: Most everyone knows something about angels, well, at least at the sentimental level through greeting cards, songs, and poetry. But are angels real? Perhaps we should have asked this at the beginning, but why not here? For most people the answer centers on how they view the Bible. The Bible plainly states: Abraham, Jacob, Moses, Joshua, Gideon, David, Elijah, Zachariah, Joseph, Mary, Peter, and others all saw angels. Is this enough proof for you? Have these very human stories in this book convinced you? In order to believe, you need to have some measure of faith.

CHAPTER 89

DEBRA'S ANGELIC PROTECTION

*D*ebra had become desperately sick—so ill that she slipped into a coma, which lasted a number of days. After her recovery she recounted the following incident.

In the middle of her coma, in her mind, in her dream, in her vision—you pick which one—she vividly saw a bright, beautiful being who appeared to be made of light. This being was beyond description. Then he spoke, "Stay with your boys; we don't need you here now!" Then it just disappeared, and she came out of her coma and made a complete recovery.

Her husband, Tim, who was at her bedside when this incident happened, saw her reach both hands heavenward in an act of worship or acceptance. It was at that point when she opened her eyes.

You know, you can pick such events all to pieces by attempting to apply logical thinking to them. You can explain them away, but to the people who experience them, like Debra, you can't take the experience away.

Debra has yet one more fascinating story:

For a little more than six years she was commuting from Springfield to the neighboring town of Republic to fulfill her responsibilities as a school teacher. The road she always took is a four-lane highway with turn lanes and stoplights.

She was stopped in the middle lane between the right hand car and one in the left turn lane, waiting for the light to change. Barreling toward the intersection, as the light changed to red, was a bright red, out-of-control, fully loaded eighteen-wheeler! It smashed into the car that had been in the turn lane making a left turn and then into a second car. The truck tipped on its side, pushing the two cars ahead of it, and skidded at a high rate of speed directly toward Debra and her car!

She seemed to have no other choice but to prepare herself for a crash. And so she did. She shouted, "Jesus! Make it stop!"

All of a sudden a huge hand appeared between Debra and the oncoming truck that was pushing the smashed cars toward her. Then the strangest, most wonderful thing happened. This smashed up mess—two cars and a semi with its trailer—came to an absolute halt not more than three or four inches from her car! Gas and oil spills were covering the highway and making a real fire danger possible. She scrambled out of her car, ran to the shoulder out of harm's way, and stood there giving praise to God for protection.

How had it happened? The truck driver had fallen asleep at the wheel and lost control. The highway patrol quickly arrived on the scene and took it all in. He spoke to Debra, "Lady, it is some kind of a miracle that you were not struck by the careening truck. I can't believe it. How did you survive?" So she recounted the events as she remembered them.

He then replied, "There is no other explanation for this truck coming to such a quick and sudden stop. Do the angels always ride with you?"

Oh, yes, I almost forgot, the two other car drivers and the truck driver all escaped injury; they were just shook up a bit. The patrolman could hardly believe his eyes and told her, "To have such extensive damage and no injuries is impossible. It had to be some kind of divine interference."

Suddenly an angel of the Lord appeared and a light shone in the cell. He struck Peter on the side and woke him up. "Quick, get up!" he said, and the chains fell off Peter's wrists. Then Peter came to himself and said, "Now I know without a doubt that the Lord sent his angel and rescued me from Herod's clutches and from everything the Jewish people were anticipating" (Acts 12:7,11).

FOOD FOR THOUGHT: Angels are beings of action! One struck Peter and if I know Peter, he was probably a deep sleeper. He woke Peter and commanded, "Quick! Get up!" Their actions can happen quickly. Intervention can happen in mere seconds. Now that thought is incredible. How can they get from heaven to earth and know their orders in less time than it takes to tell this story? Maybe someday we will be privileged to understand.

CHAPTER 90

OH NOOOOO!

*J*unetta Fields of Kansas City, Missouri, had a very strange experience. Let's let her tell it in her own words:

A year ago, as was my normal habit, I went to bed about 10:00 p.m. Everything seemed to be normal. Nothing was happening out of the regular routine to indicate to me that this night would hold something strange. I fell asleep as usual.

About 2:00 a.m., I was awakened, but at first I didn't open my eyes. The strangest sensation began—it was as though I were dying. It seemed as if my breath was being drawn out of my body. It's difficult to put it into words. My breath was being drawn out of my body and suspended just out of reach of my arms. Air was steadily being sucked out of my lungs. It was as if an evil presence was intent on taking my life. I just knew I was dying. But I also remember thinking, "If this is what it is like to die, this is not too bad. It's quite pleasant."

More time went by and the drawing away of my breath continued. Then I thought to myself, *I am not supposed to be dying because I haven't done what I was put on this earth to accomplish.*

And all the while, my breath was being taken away, and I sensed the end was quite near. I was about to pass out and enter eternity when all of a sudden I noticed two angels near my head—one on each side. I sensed their presence, opened my eyes, and saw two bright beings. I was sure they were angels sent on a mission. I just knew it in my mind and spirit.

One turned in my direction and said, "Oh, no!" It was emphatically said, but it was also drawn out and sounded something like this, "Oohhhh, Nooooo!" It was like a command as though this angel was making sure death did not come to me!

Immediately my breath came back into my body, and I was able to breathe normally once again. I was zapped back into my body. It had been a frightening experience, yet at the same time, not an experience that caused me fear.

During those moments it seemed to me as though the angels or my guardian angel had forgotten to be on duty. It was as if he had been assigned to take care of me and protect me against the enemy of my soul who wanted to kill me, but for a short period of time, he had been distracted. It seemed as though he had forgotten to watch over me and suddenly had remembered.

I began to praise and thank the good Lord for His mercy and deliverance. And I thought about this experience, how it happened and what it could have meant.

With the reassurance of the presence of the two angels, I went back to sleep and slept the night through like a baby. I awoke in the morning strangely energized and in the best health of my life. Not only had there been protection, but my spirit and body were refreshed!

> *But even the archangel Michael, when he was disputing with the devil about the body of Moses, did not dare to bring a slanderous accusation against him, but said, "The Lord rebuke you!"* (Jude 9)

FOOD FOR THOUGHT: I am always fascinated at the great variety of angelic encounters. Junetta experienced something beyond the normal sleep most of us experience, and I think it was a look into the spiritual world. From the above verse we can see that the devil is on the alert, ready to snatch away any servant of the Lord he can. But notice, Michael and the Lord were victorious!

CHAPTER 91

AN ANGEL LOOKALIKE?

*H*ow did this stranger know his name? Burton Pierce was puzzled. This day had been one of a series of unusual happenings, and now this was the strangest of them all.

On Friday, August 15, 1969, Burt, with his wife, his mother, and a grand-niece had decided to drive from a town in Upper Michigan to Duluth, Minnesota, about 100 miles away. They took the scenic route, which bordered Lake Superior, instead of a more direct one.

After stopping for lunch, they continued driving along the Red Cliff Indian Reservation. About 2:00 p.m., after traveling a short distance past a small roadside park, Burt was strangely and strongly impressed to turn around and return to the park. His passengers questioned his strange decision, but he followed this very strong impulse.

They got out of the car and sat down at a picnic table to rest and wait. Quickly, a man emerged from another part of the park. Clearly it was evident he had been crying.

Burt tells us what happened:

He walked directly toward me and after a few seconds said, "You're Burt, aren't you?"

I didn't know how he knew my name, but I was so concerned about the man that I put my curiosity aside. We sat down facing each other, and he poured out his heart. Part Native-American, Bill spilled out the tragic story of an auto accident that happened while he was driving in Oregon. His wife and only daughter had died when the car plunged into a canyon. He was so overcome with remorse and loneliness he had planned to take his own life that day.

I encouraged Bill to look to the Savior who could meet his needs. I shared some of God's Word with him. I prayed with him, and Bill opened his heart and invited Jesus Christ to come into his troubled life.

Then I realized why I had felt this strong impression to turn around and come to this remote roadside park. But one thing puzzled me, so I asked Bill, "How did you know my name?" I thought perhaps we had met before.

He looked at me strangely. "Why, don't you remember?" he asked. "We were talking this morning down in the lower park."

"But Bill," I said, "I was a long way from here this morning."

"No, Burt, it was you. It looked just like you, except you had on a different colored sport shirt. And you told me to come to the upper part of the park and wait for you."

I assured him it couldn't have been me and told him where I had been that morning, visiting my mother in Upper Michigan.

Then he looked at me and asked, "Well, where are you from?"

"I live in Springfield, Missouri," I told him.

He immediately replied, "You told me this morning that you were from Missouri!"

All of those who participated in this strange encounter later became convinced that the person Bill had met that morning must have been an angelic messenger sent to keep Bill from his plans of suicide until Burt could talk and pray with him to invite the Savior into his life. It turned out that Bill had been waiting hour after hour for God's human messenger to arrive!

During the night Paul had a vision of a man of Macedonia standing and begging him, "Come over to Macedonia and help us" (Acts 16:9).

FOOD FOR THOUGHT: How about that? An angelic lookalike! Haven't you been interested in the variety of ways, recorded in this little book, in which angelic visitors have ministered and appeared? God is unlimited in the methods He uses to accomplish His purposes.

A FINAL NOTE

When you go to the Bible for your research and insight into angels, you will not be disappointed! The Bible is full of stories about them! More than half—34 to be exact—of the Bible's 66 books mention angels and often in great detail. Every writer of the New Testament affirms the existence of angels. This is obviously not some minor, obscure subject which is hidden so only biblical scholars can unearth it.

Maybe the most important fact to keep in mind is that Jesus Christ talked about angels as being real and involved in many phases of human activity. He even stated He could have called legions of them to come to His rescue. So we are not talking or writing about beings that are figments of fertile imaginations.

I should note one more thing about angels—the Bible divides them into two groups: the holy angels of God who do His bidding, and the angels who followed Satan as he rebelled against God. The number of evil angels are said to have been about 1/3 of the total. Therefore, good angels are twice as numerous and by inference twice as powerful as the messengers of evil. That is a truth not told by many so called "angel guides." In fact, they may lead you into an encounter with an "angel" who is out to destroy you! This is the reason why the Word of God is so important. Your knowledge of God's Word will be your best protection against the deceptions of Satan or any of his evil angels. Discipline yourself to be discerning in this area.

And if you are a person who has experienced angelic experiences, why not share it with others. Your story may be the blessing and encouragement somebody else needs!

About the Author

ROBERT STRAND is the author of more than 60 books, which have sold more than five million copies. A consummate storyteller, Robert knows how to blend the emotional impact of true stories with practical insights from his many years of pastoral experience to produce breakthrough results. He and his wife, Donna, live in Springfield, Missouri.